Contents

Introduction   5
Peter Catterall   11

Part I: Gladstone, Liberalism and Ireland   9

Gladstone and Liberalism
Paul Adelman   11

Parliamentary Reform in the 1880s
Martin Pugh   18

Gladstone and Ireland
Edgar Feuchtwanger   27

Parnell and Home Rule
Donald MacRaild   35

Britain and Ireland 1880–1921
Christopher Collins   44

Part II: Disraeli, Conservatism and Empire   51

Disraeli: Political Outsider
Robert Blake   53

Tory Democracy
Bruce Coleman   61

'Juggler Joe': Radical and Unionist
Duncan Watts   66

Brits, Boers and Blacks: The Boer War 1899–1902
Keith Surridge   75

Part III: Labour, New Liberals and the Descent to War   83

New Unionism
Peter Catterall and Joyce Howson   85

The Origins of the ILP
David Howell   93

New Liberalism and Social Reform
Duncan Tanner   102

Votes for Women
Martin Pugh   109

British Foreign Policy 1894–1914
Sam Merry   114

Examiner's Report
Jessica Saraga   122

Introduction

Britain has a long history of parliamentary representation. The idea of Parliament as the forum of the nation, and of parliamentary debate as the cockpit of its politics, was a powerful one, even for those excluded from the Parliamentary franchise in the nineteenth century. There were parliamentary debating societies, which aped in detail the procedures of the Commons, amongst radical circles at the time of the Great Reform Act. Many early Labour MPs cut their debating teeth in such bodies. There was even a 'Parliament' at Newnham College, Cambridge before the First World War, despite the fact that the ladies who attended the college were not then eligible to vote in parliamentary elections.

Women, nevertheless, did gain the vote at various levels of local government from 1869 onwards. This was justified by seeing the concerns of local authorities as an extension of traditional female responsibilities for the welfare of the family. Electing a Parliament responsible for law and order, defence and the maintenance of the Empire was for many an entirely different matter. Most mid-Victorians, both male and female, believed that this was a separate sphere for which women were not suited. There were also fears that if women did attain the vote they might use it for their own interests, rather than to serve the interests of the nation. Finally, but by no means least important, there was the problem of which party would benefit if electoral reform was enacted.

These last two considerations also operated whenever further extensions of the franchise for men were debated. Democracy in 1867 was still seen as a means of passing control from the responsible to the self-interested sections of society, and Disraeli made it clear that he had no intention of doing such a thing. The Reform Acts of 1867 and 1884 were not seen as advancing democracy, although it was appreciated that they tended in that direction. Disraeli instead chose to describe 1867 as the grant of 'popular privileges'. In effect this conveys the impact of both pieces of legislation; the granting of the privilege of the vote to new groups, rather than treating the vote as a right for all. The result was a fiendishly complicated qualification system in which the task of the election agents of the parties was not so much to canvass the electorate, as to ensure their supporters were on the register and appeal against the registration of those of the other side. It was a system which essentially remained based on the occupation of qualifying properties or dwellings. It used to be argued that this system was heavily biased against the working class, and thus against the Labour Party which emerged after 1900. However, whilst there was certainly a small bias (though significant in some constituencies) in favour of propertied plural voters, the working classes do not seem to have been differentially excluded. The unenfranchised were the young of all classes, who did not yet occupy properties in their own right. The working class proportion of the electorate after 1884 was only slightly less than their weight in the population as a whole.

The working class, meanwhile, formed an increasingly cohesive social group. A maturing industrialised economy encouraged this growing cohesion. It was marked by attempts from the mid-nineteenth century to form local trades councils and, in 1868, by the advent of the Trades Union Congress. Another factor was the impact of legislation upon the trade unions. For instance, in 1871, dissatisfaction with the Criminal Law Amendment Act led the TUC to create its Parliamentary Committee as its central body, to press for unions interests in Westminster. Co-ordination of trade union activity, however, remained weak. It was not until the Edwardian period that there were the first national strikes in major industries such as coal or railways. There were, however, successive strike waves in 1871–74, 1887–91 and 1911–13. Strikes and concomitant unionisation was matched by the efforts of the employers to organise themselves in defence, including the setting up of blackleg labour organisations such as the National Free Labour Association in 1893.

These strike waves coincided with falls in the rate of unemployment, which fluctuated continually in this period and prove as potent a source of social tension as industrial conflict. In particular were the unemployed demonstrations of the 1880s and 1900s. The celebration of Queen Victoria's diamond jubilee in 1887 coincided with the 'Bloody Sunday' riots in Trafalgar Square that November. Social conflict and the rise in the 1880s of the Social Democratic Federation, the organisers of the demonstrations, worried those like Lord Salisbury, who feared that socialist politics would lead to the expropriation of property. Yet the forces for social cohesion and Conservatism were just as strong. The 1880s saw the foundation of the Conservative Primrose League, as well as of socialist parties such as the SDF. It is instructive to note that the membership of the Primrose League in Bolton, a bastion of nineteenth century working class Conservatism, almost approached the total membership of the SDF in 1900.

There were forces for social integration which countered and contained the tensions caused by the rise of socialist and working class politics. The monarchy was one, the massive and enthusiastic crowds which turned out for the jubilee of 1887 and 1897 outnumbering any radical demonstrations of the period. Parliament has not usually been, but should be counted as another, its centrality to the body politic acknowledged by all but a small fraction of the still tiny socialist movement.

The period, moreover, was characterised by steady improvement as much as by conflict. Government, as well as Parliament, was reformed and its competence steadily extended. Despite the spread of the railways and the penny post, society, political culture and the provision of public welfare remained highly localised. Extensions to government competence, therefore, took place at the local as much as at the central level. Consequently, local government expenditure tended to rise more rapidly than that of central government, despite growing defence spending, particularly during the Edwardian period. Legislation gave or extended local authorities' responsibility for sanitation, for ensuring food quality, and for education and enabled them to provide services such as gas, water or tramways. As a result, by 1914 most urban housing had gas supplies and about half had water closets in place of the old communal privy middens.

Ensuring the effectiveness of legislation required a growing professionalisation of services. For instance, the increasing utilisation of doctors by Poor Law authorities and as Medical Officers of Health, led to the setting up of the General Medical Register in 1858. However, it took until 1902, partly because of medical opposition, to secure the registration of midwives.

The state was not only becoming more professional and omnicompetent in the services it provided. It was also becoming more intrusive, and the relationship between it and the individual or family was shifting. For instance, the Prevention of Cruelty to Children Act 1889 gave courts the power to remove children at risk from parental control. These developments and the growing tax base that made them possible, provided the basis for further reform under the Liberals after 1906.

In the mid-nineteenth century it was, however, still assumed that the state had at best a limited role to play in social welfare. What activity occurred was mainly in the field of sanitation or through the safety net of the Poor Law. In part the evolution from this was an incremental process of administrative reform and extensions, witnessed, for instance, by successive improvements to ineffective pieces of legislation. This, in itself, suggested the ameliorative potential of the state. From the 1880s this notion was increasingly common currency to all the parties. The idea of state involvement in social welfare was also encouraged by the economic pressures of the period. Social welfare, for the National Efficiency movement of the turn of the century, could be the means to improve British competitiveness. For New Liberals, it was a means to secure minimum conditions alongside the Poor Law. The new Labour Party, meanwhile, talked of large-scale socialisation as a way of tackling unemployment and removing the profiteering and inefficiencies of supply felt to exist under capitalism.

Few would have gone so far. However, the economic circumstances which led to the formulation of such a programme were certainly an important factor in encouraging the growth of the state in these years.

PART I
Gladstone, Liberalism and Ireland

In 1867, despite Disraeli's best efforts, the Liberal Party remained the natural party of government in Britain. This was confirmed by the substantial majority they won in the general election the following year. The succession of Gladstone to Palmerston's position, however, began to undermine the dominance of the Liberal electoral coalition. The reforms Gladstone's ministry introduced in 1868–74 went too far for some, though not far enough for others. For instance, both Nonconformists and Anglicans had cause for dissatisfaction, for very different reasons, with the 1870 Education Act. Reforms in the field of trade union legislation, did not give trade unionists all the security they had hoped for, whilst doing little to retain the support of the commercial classes. The Irish legislation also backfired, the Liberals losing some 50 seats to a new Home Rule party in the subsequent 1874 general election.

At the same time there were signs that the salience and popularity of Gladstonian financial management was coming to an end. Gladstone's financial policy was based upon low taxes and cheap government. One way to cheap government was to ensure more efficient government. The arrival of a reforming and economically minded Prime Minister led at last to the implementation of the Northcote–Trevelyan Report of 1854. Gladstone was, in 1870, able to introduce entry to the Civil Service by competitive examination, not so much as a democratic but as a meritocratic measure to ensure the dominance of Whitehall by a disinterested Oxbridge-educated élite. However, the main route to cheaper government was through reductions in defence expenditure, which remained the largest item in the Budget. It was this end, as much as the replacement of purchase of commissions with more meritocratic means of advancement, that lay behind Cardwell's army reforms of 1871. Gladstonian finance rested upon low defence costs. However, the outside world was beginning to seem more threatening, not least the economic and military rise of Germany. At the same time fiscal parsimony was seen as leading to the incompetence in Britain's first line of defence, the navy, which was damned in the Royal

Commission report of 1872. In response there were the first signs of movement away from Cobdenite free trade towards the idea of a strong and economically united empire, a wind of change Disraeli was quick to catch in his speeches in 1872. This not only furthered the shift of the middle classes towards the Conservatives, but also impacted upon attitudes towards Ireland. To the anti-Irish prejudices that were particularly strong in counties with high rates of Irish immigration, such as Lancashire, were added economic and strategic objections to the dismemberment of the United Kingdom that Gladstone was to propose in the 1880s.

Meanwhile, the trend this started towards higher defence expenditure, was to destroy Gladstonianism. Gladstone himself was eventually to resign from his fourth ministry over the naval estimates. The fractious Rosebery government that succeeded him collapsed after being defeated in the Commons on a motion censuring the War Office for inadequate supplies of cordite. The diminishing success of the Liberals was marked by the fact that both of these were minority governments. By then a combination of the redundance of Gladstonianism and Ireland had ensured that the Liberals had ceased to be the natural party of government.

Paul Adelman
Gladstone and Liberalism

The Victorian Liberal Party stood and fell by the performance of one person.
Paul Adelman gives a succinct overview of Gladstone's political career, and
describes the influences that formed his political ideas.

For most people interested in British politics the name of Gladstone is
synonymous with Liberalism and the Victorian Liberal Party. Yet
Gladstone in fact began his political career in the 1830s as the most
reactionary of Conservatives. Indeed, as a young MP he opposed practically every reform introduced by the Whig governments — from the
abolition of slavery throughout the British Empire to the introduction
of the Factory Laws. In the 1840s and early 1850s, however, Gladstone
began to move away from this youthful High Toryism towards what
we can begin to call Liberalism, even though he remained officially a
Conservative until he joined Palmerston's government in 1859. Even
after that date, as recent historians have stressed, Gladstone was never
able to shake off completely the influence of his early Tory beliefs.

The Christian politician

Why did these profound changes in Gladstone's political outlook take
place? As so often, Gladstone gave his own answer in old age when he
said: 'I was brought up to dislike and distrust liberty. I learned to
believe in it. That is the key to all my changes.' What we can discern in
the 1840s and 1850s are three great liberating influences which
together began to push Gladstone in a liberal direction. The first is
what can best be called Gladstone's conception of religious freedom.
In 1837, as a young Tory and High Churchman, he had written to his
friend Henry Manning, later the Roman Catholic Cardinal, suggesting
that for him the main problem of politics at the time was 'how the principle of Catholic Christianity is to be applied to the conduct of public
affairs'. This could only be achieved, Gladstone then believed, through
the union of Church and State and therefore an acceptance of the special rights and privileges that belonged to members of the Established
Church of England.

In the 1840s, however, this belief collapsed. Gladstone now came to
feel that what the Church of England needed if it was to perform its
religious function effectively was less rather than more association
with the State; in effect he came to accept the great liberal ideal of 'a

free church in a free state'. But once he demanded freedom for the Church of England he found himself logically impelled to demand it for other creeds and sects too. The acceptance of this new conception of religious freedom was symbolised by his vote in 1847 in favour of admitting Jews to the House of Commons; and it was thereafter a conviction which governed his whole political life. In the 1880s, for example, Gladstone supported the claims of the notorious atheist, Charles Bradlaugh, to enter the House of Commons, even though he personally detested everything that Bradlaugh stood for.

The second great influence in liberalising Gladstone's outlook was that of the Conservative Prime Minister, Sir Robert Peel. In Peel's great ministry of 1841–46 Gladstone was first at the Colonial Office and then President of the Board of Trade, responsible for carrying out the details of Peel's ambitious commercial programme. For Gladstone, Peel became the ideal of a statesman and Prime Minister. What he admired in Sir Robert was his mastery of government and administration, his assiduous leadership of the Cabinet, his devotion to the national interest, and above all his faculty for devising great schemes and programmes. What Peel presented to Parliament and the people of England was a vision of a prosperous, united Britain.

It was a vision which was based upon the Prime Minister's conception of economic freedom. This implied for Peel, as for Gladstone, a commitment to the principles of free trade and *laissez-faire*. An acceptance of the free enterprise system would lead to economic growth and prosperity for all sections of the country, including the working classes. But Gladstone's commitment to economic liberalism did not mean that he relished any weakening in the power of government: far from it. Like Sir Robert Peel, he believed in strong leadership and an efficient, purposeful and active Executive. As he said years later in the 1870s:

> My opinion is and has long been that the vital principle of the Liberal Party is action, and that nothing but action will ever make it worthy of the name of a party.

A third important factor that influenced Gladstone in the 1850s was the principle of nationality. It first became important to him in connection with Italy, to which he was drawn by virtue of his knowledge of and interest in her language, history and culture. Italy at this time was still divided up into a number of states often ruled by oppressive and corrupt governments. After a visit there in 1851 Gladstone became more and more sympathetic to the cause of Italian unity and liberty. It was a theme which was to emerge again in connection with the 'Bulgarian Agitation' in 1876, and even more so during the campaign for Irish Home Rule during the following decade.

It was in fact the Italian question — on which the two men saw more or less eye to eye — that helped Gladstone to overcome his suspicions of Lord Palmerston, whose foreign policy he had bitterly denounced a generation earlier, and join his new government in 1859. Gladstone, who had been a leading member of the tiny group of Peelites after the break-up of the Conservative Party in 1846 over the repeal of the Corn Laws, was now prepared to throw in his lot with Liberalism and the Liberal Party as it eventually became in the 1860s. But it was not just Italy that drove him to make the final break. Apart from a brief spell as Chancellor of the Exchequer in the early 1850s in Aberdeen's Whig–Peelite coalition, Gladstone had been out of office since his membership of Peel's ministry of 1841. He was profoundly conscious of his own ambitions and abilities. He noted in his Diary: 'I have great things to do', and for this membership of a strong government was essential. The year 1859 marks, therefore, the beginning of Gladstone's great period of constructive reform which lasts until roughly 1872, by which time he had himself become Prime Minister following the great Liberal election victory in 1868. What, then, were the achievements of this period of reform?

What Gladstone would probably have considered his most notable achievement lay in the field of finance, a subject that dominated his ministerial work as Chancellor of the Exchequer in the 1860s. Gladstone aimed at what he later called 'sound and straight' finance. This meant an efficient Treasury controlling the nation's finances in a strict and methodical way; a policy of 'retrenchment' (a favourite Gladstonian word), that is, cutting down on government expenditure, especially on the armed services; and low taxation, thus allowing money 'to fructify in the pockets of the people'. Gladstone's great hope was to abolish the income tax completely, something he was never quite able to achieve. On the other hand, in the wider sphere of commercial taxation he largely completed Peel's free trade programme. Gladstone believed that his financial and commercial reforms would strengthen the economy and produce prosperity for all classes, and thus help to ensure greater social harmony. Gladstone was to buttress rather than undermine the mid-Victorian social and political system. In so far as Gladstone had a 'programme' of reform, it was one that was applied *before* rather than after he became Prime Minister in 1868.

The people's statesman

Gladstone's work for the Liberal Party in the 1860s and early 1870s was concerned as much, if not more, with matters outside rather than inside the House of Commons. For he was no narrow parliamentarian. He aimed to build up support for the Liberal Party among the new expanding elements in the nation at large. He appealed to two groups in particular: first, the skilled working classes who were becoming more prosperous and powerful through the growth of the mid-Victorian economy, and secondly, the influential and expanding religious communities of the nonconformists. To win them over Gladstone quite deliberately used the publicity resources of the time: the great mass meeting, which he made peculiarly his own especially in the industrial areas; and the Press, where he made sure that his speeches were reported in detail.

Why this concern with the working classes? One factor that influenced him enormously was the fortitude of the Lancashire cotton operatives during the 'cotton famine' of 1861–65, a direct consequence of the American Civil War. Despite their sufferings, as Gladstone noted with increasing respect, the cotton workers continued their support for Lincoln and the North even though it was the latter who, through their naval blockade of the Southern Confederacy, were the instruments of the widespread distress in Lancashire. Other evidence pushed him in the same direction. He was impressed by the growing respectability and responsibility of the great craft unions of the period; by the expansion of the Friendly Societies; and by the workers' use of his own savings banks scheme. The workers' attitude was now, he wrote, 'one of confidence in the law, in parliament, even in the executive government'. Hence, Gladstone's famous 'pale of the Constitution' speech in May 1864 in which he appeared to argue in favour of extending the vote to at least a section of the working classes.

As Gladstone moved out to the people, especially through his great meetings in the North during the electoral campaign of 1865, when, as he said in a famous remark, he appeared amongst them 'unmuzzled', so the working classes came to see Gladstone as the one statesman who appeared to speak for them and their aspirations. As a delegation of Yorkshire textile workers wrote to him:

> We have marked your manifestations of sympathy with the downtrodden and oppressed of every clime … these acts and speeches make up a life that commands our lasting gratitude.

We can see a similar rapport developing between Gladstone and the nonconformists. 'A liberal and kindly treatment of the Church of England by the State and of the Dissenters by the Church is what I desire,' he said. The nonconformists came to see Gladstone as the great Liberal statesman who accepted their fundamental demand for civil equality and supported their specific demands — the abolition of the payment of church rate and the opening up of Oxford and Cambridge to non-Anglicans, for example. Above all, they regarded him as a man who had the same profound belief as themselves in the moral basis of politics.

The importance of all this is enormous. What Gladstone helped to achieve in the 1860s and early 1870s was to win over to the Liberal Party the vast majority of the skilled working classes, who received the vote by the Second Reform Act of 1867, and the bulk of the nonconformists. In this way he helped to make the Liberal Party a national party, and indeed a classless party, which aimed to appeal to all classes and thus help to reduce the barriers between them. This point serves to underline the way in which Gladstone led the Liberal Party. For one of the main problems that faced the Liberals during this, and indeed later, periods, was how to maintain unity within a party which was more or less a coalition of different groups and interests; workers and employers, Whigs and Radicals, Nonconformists and Anglicans. Unity was maintained not through political organisation, not even through political programmes, but primarily through Gladstone's claim to be 'above' the Liberal groups by virtue of his links with the masses.

Achievements in office

Gladstone's final and best known achievement during his years in office after 1859 were the outstanding reforms of his First Ministry during the period between 1868 and 1872, though (as has been suggested above) they did not amount to a coherent programme and, with the exception of one or two Irish reforms, Gladstone had no great personal commitment towards them.

One important part of this legislation is institutional reform, such as the well-known reforms of the army, civil service, local government and the courts of law. Here the aim was primarily efficiency and economy. Another group of reforms were concerned with religious equality, notably those which granted the nonconformists most of what they had demanded, as described above. Some topics for reform were already in effect in the pipeline when Gladstone took over as Prime Minister, and their details were hammered out as a result of the clashes and compromises between the government and the special interests involved. The two best examples of this are the Education Act of 1870 and the Trade Union Act of 1871. Other important legislation was concerned with Ireland; the Irish Church Act of 1869 and the Land Act of 1870. The former, with its proposals for disestablishing and disendowing the Anglican Church of Ireland was almost wholly successful; the latter only partially so.

Alongside this domestic legislation we may also place the characteristic themes of Gladstonian foreign policy. Here Gladstone's fundamental principle was his commitment to the notion of the 'law of nations'; a public law overriding selfish national interests and committing the nations of the world to work together for peace and mutual understanding. It was on this basis that he had earlier attacked the foreign policy of Lord Palmerston. Now he used the same idea to support the 'Alabama' Award to the United States, and oppose the claim of Prussia to Alsace-Lorraine.

By 1873, however, symbolised by Gladstone's failure to pass his Irish Universities Bill, the Liberal government was clearly running out of steam. Gladstone after five years in office was now finding it extraordinarily difficult to maintain the unity of the Liberal Party. Though there had been a real consensus within the party over the subjects of reform, the details of some of the most important pieces of legislation, notably the Education Act of 1870 which antagonised the nonconformists, led to bitter divisions and quarrels among Liberals, even within the ranks of the government itself. After 1873 it was difficult for the Liberal Party to see the way forward. As Gladstone said sadly: 'There is now no great cause, no great public object on which the Liberal Party are agreed and combined.' Disraeli put the same point more pithily and no less accurately: 'the Liberal Cabinet are a range of exhausted volcanoes'.

By the beginning of 1874 Gladstone was disillusioned with his colleagues and his party, and prepared therefore to welcome a general election. The result was a remarkable triumph for Disraeli and the Conservatives. For Gladstone the defeat represented not only the collapse of that rapport with the masses which he had earlier built up, but a betrayal by his party. In the following year, therefore, he resigned the leadership of the Liberal Party.

> I felt myself to be in some measure out of touch with some of the tendencies of the Liberal Party, especially in religious matters. I deeply desired an interval between parliament and the grave.

It was not to be. Within a year, in 1876, Gladstone re-emerged into active politics to assume the leadership of the Bulgarian Agitation directed against Disraeli's Eastern policy. It marked the beginning of a new current in his political life which was to sweep him forwards to the resumption of the Liberal leadership, the great electoral victory of 1880, and the formation of his Second Ministry.

Gladstone's legacy

But the years after 1880 were a largely sterile period for the Liberals, partly because of the Grand Old Man's obsession with Home Rule for Ireland. This meant that he continued as leader of the party until 1894, when he was well into his eighties. This longevity made it ever more difficult for the Liberals to adapt to the new domestic problems of the later years of the nineteenth century, which were concerned more with the social and economic conditions of the working classes than with religious or constitutional issues. It is no coincidence, therefore, that two years after the death of Gladstone in 1898 a new political party was formed which, unlike the Liberals, did claim to be a class party, the party of the working class. That party was the Labour Party; and its formation is an instructive comment on the weaknesses and failures of the last phase of Gladstonian Liberalism.

Further Reading

Feuchtwanger, E.J. *Gladstone*, 2nd edn. (Macmillan, 1989).

Matthew, H.C.G. *Gladstone 1809–1874* (Oxford University Press, 1986).

Shannon, R. *Gladstone*, Vol. 1, 1809–1865 (Methuen University Paperback, 1984).

Vincent, J. *The Formation of the Liberal Party 1857–1868* (Constable, 1966).

Paul Adelman is the author of several books, including *The Decline of the Liberal Party*.

Martin Pugh
Parliamentary Reform in the 1880s

The parliamentary reforms of the 1880s marked an important stage in the transformation of British politics in the nineteenth century. The major extension of the franchise that resulted was only one of a number of significant consequences.

The 1880s saw three major measures of parliamentary reform: the Corrupt and Illegal Practices Act of 1883, the 'Third Reform Act' of 1884, and the Act to redistribute parliamentary constituencies of 1885. In a sense all three may be regarded as consequences of the 1867 Reform Act. An illogical measure patched together to suit a variety of conflicting interests, it was never likely to be more than a temporary expedient to meet the needs of the government of the day.

For many politicians, the Second Reform Act had the effect of intensifying a long-standing conviction that the most desirable type of reform was that designed to curtail the corruption associated with popular elections. A series of measures were indeed passed in 1854, 1868 and 1872 for this purpose, but all seemed inadequate and ineffective. Some advocates of the secret ballot, enacted in 1872, had expected this to check bribery; but in practice the ballot often enabled voters to receive payments from both sides instead of one! During the 1870s many Radical Liberals felt that the effects of franchise reform in opening up the system to wider participation were being cancelled out because the rising costs of electioneering gave a major advantage to the wealthy. The petitions presented after each election which enabled malpractice to be investigated, represented merely the tip of the iceberg (see Table 1); for where both sides were guilty, complaints were unlikely to be made. Criticism of corruption reached a head after the general election of 1880 which proved to be particularly expensive. At Bridgwater in Somerset the Commissioners who subsequently investigated the conduct of the election concluded that three-quarters of all the voters were 'hopelessly addicted' to bribery. In Bewdley in Worcestershire the Conservative candidate gave £4,000 to two agents to be spent largely on drinks for supporters dispensed at 20 public houses. And in Westminster W.H. Smith, who gained the seat from John Stuart Mill, spent no less than £9,000, much of which procured cabs to convey electors to the poll.

Parliament	Petitions presented	Successful petitions
1865	61	13
1868	51	22
1874	22	10
1880	28	16
1885	8	3
1886	3	0
1892	12	5
1895	7	1

Table1: Election petitions 1865–95.

As a result, in January 1881, the new Gladstone government announced a bill involving two basic objectives: a drastic reduction in expenditure and penalties sufficiently severe to deter malpractices. First, the legislation set a legal maximum for expenses linked to the number of voters in a constituency, the rate being much higher for counties than for boroughs. Second, it specified a list of prohibited practices including treating, bribery, undue influence, personation of voters, exceeding the expenditure limits, and paying for the transportation of voters; and it required all expenditure to be handled by a single agent for each candidate who was obliged to make a detailed return of every item within 35 days of an election. Thirdly, a number of penalties for illegal and corrupt practices were imposed ranging from fines for minor infringements to a one year prison sentence, exclusion from the House of Commons for seven years and permanent exclusion from the representation of the constituency in which the offence had been committed. Though draconian, these regulations enjoyed bi-partisan support — a recognition that all previous efforts had failed to check the rising tide of electoral malpractice.

The county franchise

Much more controversy arose over changes in both the voting qualifications and the boundaries of the constituencies during 1884–85. One can distinguish broadly three lines of explanation for these reforms. The first is that from the perspective of the Radical Liberals, franchise reform was essentially unfinished business left over from 1867. Then Disraeli had felt obliged to meet some of the Radicals' objectives by instituting qualifications for householders and lodgers, but only in the parliamentary boroughs. To have extended these to the counties would probably have provoked a revolt by backbench Tories.

But the resulting compromise was indefensible. Moreover, as the Radicals improved their organisation during the 1870s they grew increasingly conscious that they enjoyed a good deal of untapped support in the counties, both industrial ones where miners and similar groups were numerous, and rural ones where the agricultural labourers and their union leaders were enthusiastic Gladstonians. Once the questions of electoral corruption had been taken in hand, the more cautious party leaders felt fewer qualms about further reforms, though the Whigs rightly feared that the effect would be to strengthen the Chamberlainites at their expense. A second explanation is simply that after his triumphant return to office in 1880 Gladstone's government had seriously run out of steam. The Prime Minister's absorption with imperial problems, obstructionism by the Irish members, and diversions created by the Bradlaugh affair and Lord Randolph Churchill's Fourth Party meant that the opportunity to tackle the domestic issues which most concerned Radical Liberals had not been taken. For Gladstone it was therefore tempting to head off the rising Radical discontent by offering a major reform towards the end of the government's life. By making it clear that any new franchises would apply equally in Ireland, Gladstone ensured that the Nationalists would be co-operative and that his bill would obtain a comfortable majority in the Commons.

The role of the Lords

The third strand of explanation involves the Conservatives, now languishing under the dual leadership of Lord Salisbury and Sir Stafford Northcote and subject to attack by Churchill and the party organisation. The party's electoral interest seemed to dictate resistance to franchise reform, especially as Gladstone deliberately avoided making any proposals about the redistribution of the constituencies. This was partly because he knew that the Irish disliked redistribution, which would reduce their representation, and because in England the combination of a wider electorate and the old constituencies was considered certain to be damaging to the Conservatives at the next election.

In this situation Salisbury's only real weapon was to use the Conservative majority in the House of Lords to reject the franchise bill. However, the position of the Tory peers was by no means as strong as this suggests. They knew perfectly well that to persist with rejection would be dangerous. It would suit Gladstone to put himself at the head of a popular radical campaign for the franchise, hold a general election in the manner of 1880 and return with a mandate for his bill and possibly for some of the other items in the National Liberal Federation's programme. The peers were given a taste of this during the summer of 1884, following their defeat of the bill, when the

Liberals brought the whole future of the House of Lords under public scrutiny. Significantly, the peers had rejected the bill by only 59 votes. Most realised that they would have to accept a compromise. What emerged was a deal whereby they agreed to pass the franchise bill while Gladstone undertook to introduce redistribution. This was not unlike the strategy adopted by Derby and Disraeli in 1866–67: if they must take a risk on a wider electorate at least they should try to claw back some advantage by means of the new constituency boundaries. A settlement along these lines suited Gladstone, who did not want the radicals' campaign against the Lords to get out of hand, and Salisbury, who would have a respectable deal to show his party.

Redistribution of seats

As a result, a conference involving Gladstone, Hartington, Sir Charles Dilke, Salisbury and Northcote settled the details of the redistribution scheme so that it could be passed without much dissent in 1885. The new system certainly involved sweeping changes, but it is incorrect to suggest that it introduced equal-sized constituencies. At most the constituencies were made much less unequal. Only boroughs whose population was below 15,000 lost their separate representation entirely, while those between 15,000 and 50,000 lost one of their two MPs. New constituencies were created for units of population of 50,000 (see Table 2).

More striking was the decision to abolish the traditional pattern in which most borough and county seats returned two members in favour of a single-member system in all but 23 boroughs.

Seats gained:
39 in metropolitan boroughs
25 in existing English boroughs
 9 in new English provincial boroughs
64 in new English counties

Seats abolished:
14 in 7 two-member boroughs (under 15,000 population)
65 in 65 single-member boroughs (under 15,000
     population)
12 in 6 two-member rural boroughs
36 in 36 two-member boroughs which retained one
     member

Table 2: Major changes in the distribution of
constituencies in 1885.

The new boundaries were to be drawn up with regard to 'the pursuits of the people', which meant grouping together distinct economic and social interests in separate constituencies as far as possible.

This novel scheme was the result of a coincidence of interest by the two extremes — radical Liberals and Lord Salisbury. For the radicals the abolition of the two-member seats seemed likely to curtail the Whig elements in the party, and in any case, equal constituencies was a long-standing demand since the days of the Chartists. There was, in fact, an assumption that a single-member system gave results that fairly represented each party. This, as subsequent electoral history has demonstrated, was fundamentally untrue. Even in the 1880s the case for proportional representation was being made, especially on behalf of Irish Liberals now being squeezed between the extremes of Nationalism and Unionism. However, proportional representation involved multi-member constituencies, and this idea had been somewhat discredited by the experiment with three-member seats for five boroughs and seven counties introduced in 1867 as an expedient for giving Conservative representation in Liberal strongholds. Neither side had much inclination to retain the scheme, and both argued that minorities would be better represented by single-member seats.

For his part Salisbury surprisingly favoured the Radical notion of single-member seats partly because this would facilitate the long-standing Conservative objective of drawing the boundaries so as to separate the urban electorate from the Conservative, rural districts. The new system seemed likely to preserve the influence of Tory landowners more effectively than Disraeli's crude attempts at packing the boundary commissions in 1867. In the event there proved to be rather more solid Conservative communities in the 'villadom' of the new suburban constituencies; and the verdict on the redistribution of 1885 has been that Salisbury showed considerable shrewdness in the question, though at the time this was not generally appreciated.

Consequences of reform

The ramifications of the innovations of the mid-1880s spread very widely and deeply through the British political system, though there is room for debate over both the extent and the timescale of subsequent change. In any assessment it is important to distinguish the immediate effects from the indirect and long-term consequences which are much more difficult to measure.

As far as the conduct and probity of elections is concerned historians tend to share the view of contemporaries that the 1883 Act proved to be a very effective measure. At the first election expenditure was reduced by 75%. By the Edwardian period candidates typically spent about four shillings per vote compared with several pounds before

1883. The number of election petitions dropped sharply (see Table 1), though this does not mean that malpractice ceased overnight. Bribery lingered in the medieval boroughs amongst voters who had been accustomed to it in the pre-reform era. For example, when Worcester was investigated after the 1906 election the commissioners estimated that one voter in six was susceptible to corruption. However, this was now becoming an oddity and, by 1914, corruption had largely ceased to be an issue.

Two qualifications must be made. While restricting their local expenditure, the political parties steadily increased the central funds managed by the chief whips and often raised by means of the sale of peerages and knighthoods. During the twentieth century they effectively circumvented the legal restrictions by huge expenditure on national campaigns in the name of the party rather than individual candidates. Second, electioneering remained an expensive business for working-class politicians. During the 1890s, for example, the Independent Labour Party was undoubtedly handicapped by relative poverty, though finance was not an absolute bar to participation.

Party organisation

The 1883 Act had other implications for the parties. It made it imperative for any candidate who seriously hoped to win an election to obtain the services of a skilled agent who understood the law. This stimulated the development of professional bodies of full-time organisers in both parties. But it was also clear that the work of the professionals would have to be supplemented by extensive voluntary activity. This especially worried the Conservatives because hitherto they had relied heavily on paying to mobilise their support and convey it to the polls. This explains why the new Primrose League was welcomed by the party leaders; it proved to be an ideal vehicle for recruiting the male and female volunteers who kept the party machine in fighting order. For the Liberals, who were reputedly better endowed with activists, the impact was less marked. But reform reinforced the existing trend towards a greater role for the organisation outside parliament. The effects were to be seen after the Home Rule split of 1886 when the constituency activists effectively took the party with Gladstone and left the Liberal Unionist rebels high and dry.

Irish Nationalists

Perhaps the first point to be made about the franchise reform of 1884 is that it added far more voters both absolutely and proportionately than either the 1832 or the 1867 acts. The implications of this for Ireland should not be forgotten. Fears expressed by Hartington and other Whigs were soon seen to be vindicated, for at the election of 1885

Liberal representation in Ireland was eliminated. With the advantage of a wider electorate the Nationalists increased their numbers from 60 to 86 MPs, and thereafter never had fewer than 81. The new rules on redistribution had not been applied to Ireland, leaving the country with 103 MPs altogether. By the Edwardian period the average Irish seat had only half as many voters as the average English seat. In this way the Nationalists obtained a very large and virtually constant place in the British parliament until 1918 which, in 1885, 1892 and 1910, allowed them to hold the balance of power.

Party gains and losses

The effects of the reforms on the British mainland appear, at first sight, to have been slight. In spite of their unproductive period in office since 1880, the Liberals were again returned as the largest party at the 1885 general election, though they no longer had an overall majority. The Conservatives won 12 more seats while the Liberals had 20 fewer seats than before. Yet beneath the surface some major changes were already under way. In many counties Liberal candidates had gained seats traditionally held by Conservatives; this was the immediate effect of enfranchising the less affluent county householders. Conversely, the redistribution helped the Conservatives to capitalise on their growing middle-class support in the major towns, suburban districts and seaside resorts. For example, London's representation rose from 22 to 59 seats, the majority of which were filled by Conservatives. Previously radical cities like Leeds and Sheffield were now divided into five single-member constituencies, and the boundary commissioners evidently carried out their instructions by following the existing patterns of residence and business. In Leeds this produced three working-class constituencies to the south of the River Aire; the West and the South included most of the skilled artisans, while much of the Irish vote was in the East. The warehouses and offices of the business community dominated the Central division, while beyond that Leeds North comprised the salubrious middle-class districts such as Headingley. In Sheffield the class character of the constituencies was equally sharp. In Brightside and Attercliffe lay the heavy industry and the manual workers; Central division incorporated the business voters and small entrepreneurs; Hallam and Ecclesall, stretching out to the west, included the residences of the city's middle class. After 1885 Leeds North and Central and Sheffield Hallam, Ecclesall and Central were almost always won by the Conservatives. This pattern, repeated throughout the country, not only gave the party a solid basis for its huge victories in 1886, 1895 and 1900, it also accelerated the embourgeoisement of the party. While many of the rural bastions of the landed and titled figures had now become dangerous territory, the safest Tory seats were increasingly to be found in the solid suburbs.

Clearly the combination of franchise reform and redistribution created more constituencies dominated by manual workers than ever before. Yet it proved to be some time before working-class or socialist parties managed to capitalise on this. At least it was now easier for them to identify the districts in which they could hope to do well. In the examples given above, Leeds East and Sheffield Attercliffe had Labour MPs by 1906. Although four men out of every ten still failed to get on to the electoral registers, no single section or class of men was now excluded from voting. As a result there was relatively little popular pressure to reform the system so far as it affected male electors between 1885 and 1914. This had important implications for the one large sector of the population that remained absolutely excluded: women.

The women's cause

Following the presentation of a petition for women's suffrage by John Stuart Mill in 1866, suffragist MPs had introduced bills and resolutions in the Commons almost annually throughout the 1870s and early 1880s. When the franchise bill was debated in June 1884 William Woodall (Liberal) proposed an amendment to enfranchise women which was defeated by a majority of 136. This reflected the official opposition of the government. Gladstone was basically against women's suffrage on principle; but in 1884 there was an important tactical consideration too. A women's suffrage amendment provided an opportunity for the Opposition to make mischief. Of those Conservatives who voted on Woodall's amendment, 77% supported him. Had the bill gone forward to the House of Lords with this addition it would have given the peers a further excuse for rejection.

This defeat for women's suffrage has usually been seen as a major setback, and the cause has been thought to have entered a decline for the next 15 or more years. However, it is necessary to distinguish problems of political tactics from changes in opinion. When Woodall introduced the same proposal in a separate suffrage bill in November 1884 he won a majority of 21 for it. This did not mean that politicians felt very strongly on the subject, but it was certainly a sign that they were gradually being converted to the suffrage cause. During the 1880s and 1890s growing numbers of women pursued a public, political role both in local government and in the party political organisations. In some ways this activity constituted a more effective argument in favour of women's enfranchisement than direct propaganda. Women were giving proof of their competence. By enfranchising many poor and ill-educated men in 1867 and 1884 politicians had made it increasingly difficult to justify the exclusion of educated, property-owning or tax-paying women. In this perspective 1884 was less of a setback than it might appear.

Conclusion

By the Edwardian period the Liberals and Labour had concluded that the reforms of the 1880s had given too great an advantage to the Conservatives. In particular the extra scope for plural voting, which arose from the single-member system, led to some half a million plural voters by 1910. The Liberals calculated that at least 30 Conservative seats could be captured if the plural vote were abolished. However, no further reform was achieved in the years before 1914. It was frustrated by four main complications: internal party divisions over the effects of enfranchising women; the obstructionism of the House of Lords; the opposition of the Irish to any redistribution of constituencies; and speculation as to how far the Labour Party might benefit from franchise reform. Consequently, the innovations of the 1880s survived intact until a comprehensive overhaul of the electoral system was undertaken towards the end of the First World War.

Further Reading

Blewett, N. 'The Franchise in the United Kingdom 1885–1918', *Past and Present* 32 (1965).

Chadwick, M.E. 'The role of redistribution in the making of the Third Reform Act', *Historical Journal* 19, 3 (1976).

Cornford, J.P. 'The transformation of Conservatism in the late nineteenth century', *Victorian Studies* 7 (1963) .

Gwyn, W.B. *Democracy and the Cost of Politics* (Athlone Press, 1963).

Hayes, W.A. *The Background and Passage of the Third Reform Act* (Garland Publishing, 1982).

Jones, A. *The Politics of Reform 1884,* (Cambridge University Press, 1972).

O'Leary, C. *The Elimination of Corrupt Practices in British Elections, 1868–1911* (Oxford University Press, 1972).

Pugh, M. *The Evolution of the British Electoral System 1832–1987* (Historical Association pamphlet, 1988).

Seymour, C.S. *Electoral Reform in England and Wales: The Development and Operation of the Parliamentary Franchise 1832–1885* (First published 1915, reprinted by Archon Books, 1970).

Martin Pugh is Professor of Modern British History at the University of Newcastle upon Tyne.

Edgar Feuchtwanger
Gladstone and Ireland

In popular perceptions Gladstone's political career is inextricably linked to Ireland. Edgar Feuchtwanger examines how Ireland came to dominate Gladstone's policy and the nature of his achievements.

Ireland loomed so large in Gladstone's career as Liberal leader and Prime Minister that in the popular mind he has come to have a special relationship with John Bull's other island. In *1066 and All That* we are told that every time Gladstone found a solution to the Irish question, the Irish changed the question. The implication is that Gladstone sought, unselfishly and idealistically, to solve a problem that dogged the British right on their doorstep, when otherwise they were so successful in ruling much of the world and solving its problems. But the Irish, with their typical cussedness, frustrated him. Much the same point is made, more seriously, more high-mindedly and at much greater length in a celebrated classic of historical writing, J.L. Hammond's *Gladstone and the Irish Nation*, first published in 1938. Such notions invite demolition by other historians. 'My mission is to pacify Ireland' – no remark of Gladstone's has become more hackneyed in quotation. He is reported to have made it, during a brief pause in his preferred form of exercise, the felling of trees, when the Queen's commission to form his first government had been conveyed to him in 1868.[1] Gladstone's remark seems to bear out Hammond's interpretation of his motives. Some more recent historians have, however, come nearer to agreeing with Parnell when he said, just before his imprisonment in Kilmainham Gaol in 1882, that Gladstone was a 'masquerading knight errant, the pretending champion of the rights of every other nation except those of the Irish nation.'

It cannot be disputed that Ireland was of no particular concern to Gladstone in his early career. He could not, however, avoid Ireland, no more than anyone else involved in British politics in the nineteenth century. His attitude was governed by his overriding commitment to the Established Church and therefore to its Irish offshoot, the Church of Ireland. When in the 1840s Peel, faced by O'Connell's renewed agitation in Ireland for a repeal of the union, wanted to send 'messages of peace' to Ireland, Gladstone emerged as one of the leading Protestants in the Cabinet. Like many other Tories, he wanted no gestures towards Irish Catholics that would cast any doubt on the Anglican position in

Ireland. Gladstone's resignation over the Maynooth grant in 1845, the first time that Ireland played a major role in his political career, has often been interpreted as a sign of an overly tender conscience in an as yet immature politician. In fact, Gladstone had acquired so high a profile as the defender of the Anglican establishment that he could hardly reverse his position and still cling to office. It was a particularly delicate moment, when the conversion to Rome of prominent members of the Oxford Movement like John Henry Newman, was causing widespread uneasiness. Gladstone was personally so close to these events that he had to take great care not to acquire the reputation of a turncoat.[2]

Disestablishment of the Church of Ireland

In the 1860s, however, just as events and his own efforts were conspiring to make him a potential contender for the Liberal leadership, the issue of Irish Church disestablishment was coming on to the political agenda. It was a matter that went to the very roots of Gladstone's beliefs. For a long time he had been moving away from the views that he had set out in great elaboration in his book, *The State in its Relations with the Church*, in 1838.

In his review of this book Macaulay had used the famous phrase 'the rising hope of stern unbending Tories', which clung to Gladstone ever afterwards. Gladstone no longer believed that the Established Church could be the spiritual guide for the State or that full citizenship was possible only for members of that Church. When a church was faced with the choice between its temporalities as an established church and the fulfilment of its spiritual mission, then the temporalities, 'the gold', would have to be sacrificed.[3] These fundamental shifts in his position enabled Gladstone to make a public declaration in March 1865 in favour of the principle of disestablishing the Church of Ireland. It was a crucial juncture in Gladstone's political progress. It was the final straw in breaking his official link with the University of Oxford as one of its representatives in Parliament. At the same time it enhanced his rapport with a vital element among the supporters of the Liberal Party, the Nonconformists. He had to find a new seat in South Lancashire, but he was brought a step nearer to the Liberal leadership.

It was one thing to declare for the disestablishment of the Church of Ireland in principle, another to do something about it in practice. There can be little doubt that when Gladstone took up the issue in 1867 as a matter for immediate action he was acting largely for tactical political reasons. It was the issue which enabled him to pull the warring factions of the Liberal Party together after the split over parliamentary reform. It enabled him to pre-empt possible steps by the Derby-Disraeli government on the Irish Church and finally put him in a position to become the leader of the Liberals after Russell's impending retirement. Gladstone's first great Irish measure, the disestablishment of the Church of Ireland, the immediate occasion for his remark about pacifying Ireland, was therefore made possible by a change of conviction, entirely genuine and painfully arrived at, but it was actually carried out as a matter of political calculation. He always cited it as a prime example of what he regarded as his supreme political gift, a capacity for right-timing.[4] One Irish grievance, 'the alien church', as Disraeli had called it, was thus disposed of.

Land and other reforms

Others remained, most obviously the many problems connected with the Irish agrarian situation. Legislative proposals on this subject had made their appearance at Westminster well before the Fenian incidents of 1867 gave Ireland a high profile with the British public. When Gladstone as Prime Minister, having disposed of the Irish Church, turned his attention to Irish land, he aimed for a solution more comprehensive than the previously desultory attempts to help the small Irish tenant farmer. In doing so he had to set aside his own strong attachment to the principles of political economy and freedom of contract. He had to do battle with one of the most deeply held beliefs of his age, the belief in the sanctity of property. In bringing the Irish Land Act of 1870 on to the statute book Gladstone's hardest fight was with some of his own cabinet colleagues. Whigs like Clarendon and Argyll and doctrinaire Liberals like Robert Lowe felt they were being asked to sanction an unprecedented degree of interference by the state in the rights of property and in the relations between landlords and their tenants.[5] What would become the law in Ireland might spread to England, at a time when the owners of land were increasingly under attack and their political pre-eminence was threatened. In the event the Irish Land Act proved a disappointment and its ability to protect Irish tenant farmers against rack-renting and eviction turned out to be very limited. The land purchase clauses inserted in the act as a result of the advocacy of John Bright proved ineffective. Nevertheless, a first step had been taken in establishing the principle that property rights were not in all circumstances sacrosanct. Gladstone's own determination to see justice done in a particular historical situation prevailed over his adherence to the abstract principles of market economics. The fact was that the Irish peasant regarded himself as the proprietor of the soil he tilled, whatever the English law that had been imposed on him in the course of history might say.

Gladstone's third attempt to meet an Irish grievance, the Irish Universities Bill of 1873, did not even reach the statute book. Only Disraeli's refusal to take office forced the Liberal government to stay on for another nine months. In spite of the imperfect success of the Irish legislation of his first government Gladstone remained optimistic about Ireland's future as part of the United Kingdom.

At this time Gladstone had natural reasons for regretting the rise of a Home Rule Party in Ireland, largely at the expense of his own party, and to profess to see no justification for it. A few months later, in the autumn of 1877, Gladstone paid his only visit to Ireland, apart from a short trip on shore from a cruise in August 1880. Although staying mainly in some of the great country mansions of the Anglo-Irish ascendancy, he did his best to get a more general impression of the country. There is little indication that his complacency about Ireland's future was disturbed. He saw the causes of Irish discontents as religious and social, capable of being resolved within the framework of the Union. In any case, the severe agricultural depression, which was shortly to exacerbate all Irish problems, had not yet struck in its full fury. When Gladstone formed his second government in April 1880 he had, therefore, no inkling that Ireland would be a major preoccupation during the remainder of his political career. He genuinely believed that his return to office at the age of 70 would be limited in time and mainly concerned with reversing some of the grosser errors of 'Beaconsfieldism', the ogre he had so effectively attacked in his Midlothian campaign.

The Irish crisis 1880-82

By 1880 the situation in Ireland had, however, gravely deteriorated. Agrarian crime and cases of eviction, barometers for the state of the Irish countryside, had risen catastrophically. The Land League had made its appearance in Ireland and the election of 1880 had brought a hard core of Irish Nationalist members to Westminster. For both, Charles Stewart Parnell was the formidable leader. All the evidence is that Gladstone and his cabinet colleagues reacted slowly and hesitantly to this situation. Shortly after taking office they allowed the special law and order legislation for Ireland, known for short as 'coercion', to lapse. To deal with Irish agricultural distress they brought in a Compensation for Disturbance Bill, such as had often been proposed in the past, which was rejected by the House of Lords. They appointed a commission of inquiry on Irish land under Lord Bessborough, a government's traditional way of avoiding immediate action. By the autumn of 1880, however, Gladstone and his cabinet became aware of the full extent of the Irish crisis. They could not be in any doubt, certainly not after the famous 41-hour sitting of January 1881, that Parnell and his followers also had the capacity to play havoc with the conduct of business at Westminster. Yet Gladstone had initially believed that Parnell led only a small and unrepresentative group. When the

Bessborough Commission reported in December 1880, it recommended in substance the enactment of the 'three Fs', fair rents, fixity of tenure and free sale. Gladstone was thus driven, against his first inclinations and his free market principles, to legislate once more on a grand scale on Irish land. He always refused to acknowledge in public that his Land Act of 1881 enshrined the 'three Fs' and claimed that it left open an ultimate return to the free market. Gladstone had also been reluctant to return to coercion, not because he failed to see the need to enforce law and order, but because he considered it futile unless accompanied by more positive measures. This was the reason why he embarked for the second time on the great undertaking of a land act. Whatever its ultimate consequences, and it was soon to be superseded by major land purchase legislation, the Land Act of 1881, combined with coercion was, in the short term, effective in calming the Irish countryside and drawing the sting of the Land League. After the summer of 1882 the Gladstone government was granted a breathing space in dealing with the problems of Ireland.

The idea of devolution

Gladstone was aware at this time that one of the steps required to cope with the Irish situation might be the provision of more self-government. At the end of 1880 he clearly saw such a step as preferable to embarking upon another big land act. He proposed to his colleagues a system of Grand Committees of the House of Commons to deal with the three parts of the United Kingdom, combined with the establishment of devolved government. He wrote:

> I must add that besides the defeat of obstruction, and the improvement of our attitude for dealing with arrears, I conceive that Devolution may supply the means of partially meeting and satisfying, at least as far as it is legitimate, another call. I refer to the call for what is called (*in bonam partem*) Local Government and (*in malam*) Home Rule.[6]

He thus proposed to kill at least two birds with one stone, the problem of obstruction within an already overcrowded parliamentary timetable, and the demand for elected local government, in Ireland as well as in the rest of the United Kingdom. He was coming to see the Act of Union, in the form it was put on the statute book by the Younger Pitt, as a mistake and a return to something like Grattan's Parliament as desirable. The recognition of separate national identities and a concern for national self-determination had always been central to Gladstone's outlook. It has been called a feeling for religious nationality, for what was in Gladstone's view essential in national identities was a specific approach to religion, usually institutionalised in a national church, which might, as in Roman Catholic countries, be a sub-branch of a wider church. Gladstone was therefore prepared, unlike many of his contemporaries, to recognise that an Irish national-ity existed. Such a nationality did not necessarily justify a separate state. Gladstone had just demonstrated similar views in his crusade for the Bulgarians. He recognised the existence of religious nationalities in the Balkans, who were entitled to self-government and autonomy, though not necessarily to independence and separation from the larger Ottoman Empire. This feeling for nationality fitted into what has been called Gladstone's European sense, his belief that the nations of Europe were united by a common bond of Christian civilisation, which ought to regulate their behaviour and keep their divisions within bounds. Gladstone's awareness of Ireland's separate national-ity did not conflict with his confidence that her grievances could best be remedied within the framework of the United Kingdom. His own legislation, particularly the Land Act of 1881, had in fact created a win-dow of opportunity for settling the question of Irish government con-stitutionally and without disrupting the overall unity of the British state.

The decision to introduce Home Rule

When Gladstone took up the cause of Irish Home Rule in 1885 it was therefore no sudden conversion. The espousal of Home Rule was no break with his fundamental principles, comparable to the negation of his early state-church views implicit in the conversion to Irish Church disestablishment. The dividing lines were fluid between devolved local government, as proposed by Gladstone in 1880, the central board scheme proposed by Chamberlain in 1885 and accepted by Gladstone, and the Home Rule bills eventually worked out in 1886 and 1893 by Gladstone. The argument advanced in its most sophisticated form by Cooke and Vincent in *The Governing Passion*, that Gladstone took up Irish Home Rule in 1885 primarily to remain in control of the Liberal Party, is thus not convincing.[7] The fact that the Home Rule cause kept Gladstone in politics, when otherwise his retirement at this point seemed likely, was a by-product of rather than the main motive for his course of action. Moreover, the evidence does not bear out Vincent's contention that Gladstone was not committed to Home Rule when he formed his third government in January 1886. Vincent argues that he might well have given priority to his land purchase scheme, but for the circumstances of Chamberlain's resignation. On the contrary it appears that by the end of 1885 Gladstone was fully convinced that there had to be a generous, large-scale measure of Irish self-govern-ment and that he was the man to see it through. The two major factors that had driven Gladstone to this conclusion were the electoral strength of the Parnellite Party, as seen in the Irish election results outside Ulster; secondly the reports of the disturbed state of Ireland reaching him, which suggested if some form of self-government was not now granted a near-revolutionary situation would arise.[8] Both these factors may not in practice have been so clear cut, but that is how Gladstone perceived them. The desire not to be relegated from the great game of politics may have played a part in Gladstone's motives, and even more so among his family and entourage; there had always been an element of make-belief in the flirtation with retirement that had accompanied his career since 1874. After the elections of November 1885 such sentiments existed only at the margins. They pale into insignificance beside the overwhelming conviction that this was a moment of great danger and opportunity and that there was no one else who could now 'pacify Ireland'. The failure of Gladstone's attempt to get the Salisbury government to tackle the problem made it clearer than ever that only he could do it.

Old man in a hurry?

There was also a grain of truth in Lord Randolph Churchill's quip that Gladstone was 'an old man in a hurry' in 1886. The cause of Anglo-Irish relations might well have been better served by a less precipitous procedure. Gladstone left himself no time to educate British public opinion, not even his own party, only recently alienated by Parnell's support of the Tories in the general election of 1885.[9] Gladstone deceived himself about the degree of resistance his scheme would encounter. He thought in terms of colonial self-government, such as had been granted less than 20 years earlier to Canada and more recently to South Africa. The opponents of Home Rule feared the break-up of the United Kingdom itself, the establishment of a hostile state on England's very door-step in an age of growing international rivalry. Gladstone was misinformed about the position of Ulster. Those to whose advice he listened assured him that Protestant opposition in Ulster came from a small bigoted minority and would amount to little once a Dublin Parliament was in place. Gladstone deceived himself that the House of Lords would not in the end dare to oppose Home Rule once it was accepted by the Commons. A measure of self-deception may be a necessary attribute in a statesman who aspires to exceptional achievement. In his tactics in pushing ahead with his Irish proposals in 1886 Gladstone reverted to the kind of executive statesmanship Peel had practised in promoting free trade in the 1840s, but he was ultimately less successful.

The failure of 1886 kept Gladstone 'like Ulysses chained to the mast' for another eight years. He was deprived of the chance of finding an answer to the Irish question, perhaps the best chance that ever existed.

When he made a second attempt in 1893, the cards were much more heavily stacked against him. The Home Rule scheme proposed by Gladstone in 1886 was a conservative scheme. Irish nationalism was itself a sufficiently conservative and constitutional movement to make it likely that Gladstone's solution could have worked. Developments in Ireland up to the First World War also bear this out. Gladstone's failure in 1886 and the Liberal split may have had damaging consequences in a wider sense. It may well have delayed the political modernisation of Britain at a critical moment. The Liberal welfare reforms might have come sooner, the divisions of the left caused by the rise of the Labour Party might have been avoided. Such speculations, counterfactual though they are, have enough plausibility to show the magnitude of the issues at stake in 1886.

Notes

(1) Magnus, P. *Gladstone* (John Murray, 1954) p.193.
(2) Shannon, R. *Gladstone, Vol. 1; 1809–1865* (Hamish Hamilton, 1982) pp.147ff.
(3) Hammond, J.L. *Gladstone and the Irish Nation* (Longman, 1938) p.51.
(4) Feuchtwanger, E.J. *Gladstone*, 2nd edn., (Macmillan, 1989) p.143.
(5) Steele, E.D. *Irish Land and British Politics. Tenant-Right and Nationality 1865–1870* (Cambridge University Press, 1974) pp.200ff.
(6) Matthew, H.C.G. Introduction to *The Gladstone Diaries*, Vol. 9 (January 1875–December 1880) (Oxford University Press, 1986) p.xxviii.
(7) Cooke, A.B. and Vincent, J. *The Governing Passion: Cabinet Government and Party Politics in Britain 1885–86* (Harvester, 1974) pp.49ff.
(8) Loughlin, J. *Gladstone, Home Rule and the Ulster Question 1882–93* (Gill and Macmillan, 1986) pp.39ff.
(9) Jenkins, T.A. *Gladstone, Whiggery and the Liberal Party 1874–1886* (Clarendon, 1988) pp.259ff.

Edgar Feuchtwanger teaches History at the University of Southampton.

Donald MacRaild
Parnell and Home Rule

In the political crisis over the question of Irish Home Rule in the 1880s Charles Stewart Parnell, whose career is analysed here, was a key figure.

The centenary of the death of the Irish nationalist leader Charles Stewart Parnell was 6 October 1991. The anniversary was marked by a BBC mini-series and a West End play. More than any other Irish leader, from Theobald Wolfe Tone to Eamon De Valera, Parnell achieved cult status in life as well as in death, and interest in both the personal and political sides of Parnell remain today. Parnell was the man who led the first truly united Irish party in the House of Commons, whilst harnessing support from the widest extremes of Irish opinion at home and abroad. His failure to achieve his ultimate objective, Home Rule for Ireland, does not seem to have diminished his reputation. Parnell's involvement in a public divorce scandal and the tragic circumstances of his premature death have become part of popular legend. This in spite of his very short political career: in 1875 he was elected as MP for Meath, by late 1891 he was dead. How, though, did Parnell the constitutionalist come to represent the aspirations of a nation whose ideas were based upon a hatred of the system of land tenure and a growing desire for political and economic self-determination? Parnell was a moderate by Irish standards and, as a landlord, he was not imbued with a hatred of that class. For the historian, Parnell, the man and the politician, represents an enigma; and it is very difficult to pin down either his true nature or the basis for his rapid progress and his enormous support.

Genesis of a Home Ruler

Little in his childhood or youth suggests that Parnell would make a great political impact. He was born on the estates of his father, John Henry Parnell, at Avondale, Co. Wicklow, on 27 June 1846. His father was a Liberal whilst his mother, Delia Tudor Stewart Parnell, was an American and an inconsistent republican, from whom he inherited a distrust of the English. His formal educational career culminated ignominiously in 1869 when, after involvement in a drunken escapade, he was rusticated from Magdalene College, Cambridge. During the early 1870s Parnell visited America, fell in love, was jilted and drifted into politics. He was elected to Parliament in Meath in 1875. Parnell's background within the Irish Protestant Ascendancy was important because it amounted to what Gladstone would later designate 'advantage of birth'. Politics was always open to his class; whilst his Protestantism gave the land reform and Home Rule campaigns a dimension of respectability, his presence contradicted the commonly held belief that nationalism was the exclusive domain of Catholics.

This was a role of some importance. During the 1840s and 1850s, Irish politics had developed an increasingly militant character. The consequences of the Great Famine of the later 1840s had reinforced denunciations of English landlordism. The Young Irelanders — men like James Finton Lalor — helped to shape popular opinion of the immorality of landlordism into a philosophy and into a political campaign. The Fenians, formed in 1858, carried this campaign beyond the Irish peasants into the Irish communities of England and America, which had been greatly swollen by the Famine exodus. Fenianism affirmed the moral ascendancy of Irish suffering as well as introducing a terrorist campaign on the British mainland, especially between 1867 and 1968. Fenianism educated the Irish (their paper *The Irish People* was widely read) but sickened and frightened the English public, and gave Gladstone his desire to 'pacify' the Irish.

By the time of Parnell's election for Meath in 1875, the foundations for a parliamentary Home Rule campaign had already been laid by the Irish Tory, Isaac Butt. Butt's Amnesty Association (1868), formed to campaign for clemency for imprisoned Fenians, served to unite a very loose Irish parliamentary party with some of their extremist counterparts. This alliance was further strengthened by Butt's Home Government Association (1870). Furthermore, the 1874 general election had seen, for the first time, the return of Irish members — 59 in all — under the banner of Home Rule. Butt, though, was a weak leader and the commitment of his party was equally shaky. If the Liberals had been elected in 1874, it is likely that provision of low-ranking government posts would have diminished the resolve of the Irish Nationalist MPs.

Butt's ineffectual advance of his party's aims meant that their clearest propaganda came through the 'obstructionist' activities of a handful of Irish radicals, led by the Cavan MP, J.C. Biggar. Foremost among these men was the newly elected Charles Stewart Parnell, who immediately assumed the mantle of a radical. He campaigned in the Commons for the freedom of imprisoned Fenians and went among the Irish in Britain and Ireland, drumming up support for Home Rule. Parnell, though, despite his use of invective, was inherently a constitutionalist but, in an effort to attract support from all wings, he extolled the moderate line for his English audiences whilst maintaining, for the benefit of Irish extremists, what Conor Cruise O'Brien has superbly described as a 'vague penumbra of revolution'. Within two years he had wrested the crown from Butt's ageing head. In 1877 Parnell assumed the Presidency of the Home Rule Confederation of Great Britain; by the spring of 1880 he was the President of the Land League and held the chair of the Irish parliamentary party.

The Land League and 'New Departure'

The agricultural depression of the late 1870s provided Parnell with the ideal opportunity to achieve popular support and pre-eminence within Irish politics. Following the Great Famine, the reduced Irish population had enjoyed an increase in living standards based on improved agricultural production, but the late 1870s saw this inter-rupted. With mounting evictions and impoverishment, landlordism, once again, became the focus for agrarian violence. Michael Davitt, the ex-Fenian who was released from prison in 1877, immediately threw himself into the fray. He realised the symbiotic nature of land and pol-itics in Ireland, although he claimed not to have read Lalor until 1880. Davitt gathered support for the tenantry, encouraging the boycotting of those lands left vacant by evictions. In conjunction with the Irish-American, John Devoy, a man impressed by Parnell's Fenian rhetoric, the two sought to implement the 'New Departure': a policy of unifica-tion between Fenianism, agrarianism and constitutionalism. This plan fully capitalised on the importance of land in Ireland, both historically and politically, because, inevitably, the system of ownership featured prominently in all discussions of Ireland's future. English landlords, often absentee, and the related and alien system of land tenure, increasingly became the focus of much acrimonious debate and physi-cal force. Several times during 1879 Davitt and Devoy met Parnell and pressed him to support the union of parliamentary and extra-parlia-mentary politics. In October 1879 the National Land League was formed with Parnell as its leader. The groups that supported the Land League — Irish politicians, workers, peasants, farmers — exemplified the broad base of discontent that existed within Ireland. What is more, this loose alliance represented the fundamental basis of Parnellism.

The Land League had an appeal for Irish communities around the world. In Ireland the population, more literate now than before, was aware of the League's activities and steadily committed itself to its purpose, although support was always strongest in the West of Ireland, where economic circumstances were most dire. The body of support for the Land League was disparate, while the leadership con-tained a strong Fenian element. Accordingly, in the words of Roy Foster, 'for a parliamentarian like Parnell, his involvement in the Land League meant riding a tiger'. The League, however, gave Parnell the ultimate mandate with which he could assume control of the Irish

Parliamentary Party in the following spring. Parnellism was not made, but it was taking shape.

Land War

Over the years 1880 to 1882, economic problems of the tenantry had continued unabated — especially in the West. In 1881 the activities of the Land League, and those outside its control, resulted in horrific animal maiming and other forms of agrarian violence. So bitter was this period that it has been dubbed the Land War. Throughout these years, the balance of constitutionalism and the vagaries of extremism combined to give Parnell his sternest tests. The return, in 1880, of Gladstone's second Liberal ministry and 60 Nationalist MPs, however, promised some resolution of Ireland's plight. Gladstone's legislative remedy was a Land Bill, aimed at quelling the raging Land War. Gladstone, it has been argued, supported an appeal to the tenantry over the head of the increasingly powerful figure of Parnell, whom he did not trust. For these tenants, his land legislation promised the '3 Fs' of popular demand: fair rents; fixity of tenure; and freedom from eviction. As a sop to English opinion, however, the Land Bill was accompanied with a coercion measure.

As a result, the Coercion Act was passed in February 1881. The Act failed to impose order upon the Irish and its effects did much to negate the positive aspects of the ensuing land legislation, especially as W.E. Forster, the Irish Secretary, enforced coercion with alacrity.

As a consummate political juggler, Parnell did not reject the terms of the Land Act but called for 'test cases' to be put before the tribunals which the Act established: a clear sign that he was struggling to maintain moderation. Forster, however, believed that Parnell was trying to wreck the Act and in October 1881, under the terms of the Coercion Act, the leaders of the Land League, including Parnell, were arrested and imprisoned in Kilmainham Gaol. In all, 955 Land Leaguers followed their leaders into prison. At this point Parnell's reputation reached heroic proportions. Extremists at home called for a rent strike; a further deterioration in law and order ensued. Parnell's control would have permanently slipped had the land agitation fallen into the hands of the extremists. By the spring of 1882 the Liberal government sought a much-needed compromise with him and, in April, the so-called 'Kilmainham Treaty' was struck. The Land Act was to be amended to protect tenants in arrears, whilst Parnell agreed to campaign for acceptance of its provisions. Forster could not stomach this change to his policy and resigned; Parnell was left to juggle the factions under his nominal control.

The 'Treaty' could have been a fatal error, because the extremist wing saw it as a betrayal. However, the Fates smiled on Parnell, though not on the new Irish Secretary: on 6 May 1882, on. after arriving in Dublin to take up his new post, Lord Cavendish was murdered in Phoenix Park along with his pe. under-secretary, T.H. Burke. Public opinion was outraged. I. denounced the actions of the 'Invincibles' who claimed responsibu. Even Davitt expressed revulsion. Parnell was probably saved by the Phoenix Park Murders from a backlash by the extreme nationalist wing over his deal with the Liberals. The pendulum had, after three years, swung to constitutional methods, culminating with the replacement of the Land League in October 1882 by the Irish National League. Through a combination of good management, political manoeuvre and luck, Parnell had restrained the Fenian element and brought the tide of opinion around to his parliamentary campaign. He had also gained a measure of respect from Gladstone. Furthermore, elements of English public opinion became more sympathetic towards Parnell for the decorum and good sense he had shown in reaction to the Phoenix Park Murders.

Parnell, Gladstone and Home Rule, 1882-86

The events of 1882 marked another turning point in Parnell's career. He had never liked the extremist line and abhorred the tactics of the Land War. Ultimately, Parnell had always sought to supersede physical force nationalism by his constitutional methods. Gladstone, who no longer saw Parnell as a dangerous demagogue, now realised the futility of trying to bypass the Irish leader. Parnell was so popular that the Prime Minister believed him to represent the great majority of Catholic opinion.

There was a further strengthening of the Parnellite position in 1884–85. The 'pledge' now bound all Home Rule candidates, if elected, to the party line. The legacy of Butt had in many respects been reforged into Britain's first modern political party. In addition, the Reform Act (1884) and the Redistribution Act (1885) worked in Parnell's favour, quadrupling the electorate to 16% of adult males. This was the first time that electoral reform was applied to Ireland on equal terms to the rest of the UK. During this period Parnell clearly began to tire of Gladstone's unwillingness to adopt a policy of Home Rule, and he began to toy with the idea of an appeal to the Conservatives. Parnell, a shrewd and hardheaded politician, was aware that the constitutional balance in the Lords favoured the Conservatives. Increased disunity within the Liberal Party and some disastrous foreign policy blunders had visibly weakened the government. Parnell withdrew Irish support and Gladstone's ministry fell in June 1885. With the constitutional reforms still being put into place, no election was held and Salisbury formed a Conservative ministry.

In quick response to Parnell's support, the Conservatives pushed through the Ashbourne Act which made for a more effective and wide-ranging land-purchase scheme than that of 1881. However, neither of the two British parties was willing to declare for Home Rule. Lord Carnarvon, the architect of federalism in Canada, favoured a similar solution for Ireland and he told Parnell that the Conservatives would accept as much. Parnell was drawn to this proposal. T.P. O'Connor, the *de facto* spokesman of the Irish in Britain, had seen the Conservatives as the better bet for the Irish as early as 1883. When Parnell commanded the Irish in Britain to oppose the Liberals in the 1885 election, O'Connor, who was to win the Liverpool Scotland division, was charged with the orchestration of the campaign. There is some debate as to whether the Irish vote in Britain was as influential as some contemporaries believed. Historians such as Alan O'Day have argued that its real influence was limited, outside O'Connor's Liverpool constituency, to three others: Cockermouth, Leeds East and Manchester South West. However, the Irish did play a part in party political considerations.

This aside, the general election of 1885 saw the return of 355 Liberals, 249 Conservatives and a much larger Irish party. Parnell held the balance of power. He could deny either party office but his support for the Conservatives would only equal the total number of Liberal seats and would not create a working majority. The decision as to which party to support was made for him. Carnarvon's scheme was thrown to the wolves by the Conservative leadership and in December Gladstone's secret conversion to Home Rule was made public.

The greatest politician of his day now supported the cause for which Parnell strove. But Gladstone had to convert his party, and the public at large were opposed to the idea of splitting the union: the Conservatives, more than ever, could appeal to deep-seated racial and cultural prejudices. Gladstone's conversion also threatened to eclipse Parnell and his party. The changes of position ultimately did neither any good in political terms: the Irish, in particular, stood to lose their much-vaunted independence. The ensuing battle over Home Rule split the Liberals, with the 'Liberal Unionists' defecting under Hartington. Gladstone's Home Rule proposals went before the Commons in April 1886. They were defeated by 343 votes to 313 and he immediately petitioned the Queen for a dissolution; she grudgingly acceded. The results of the July election were a massive reverse on the question of Home Rule: 316 Conservatives and 78 Liberal Unionists were returned against 191 Gladstonian Liberals and 85 Home Rulers. In Ulster, the Orange Order for the first time demonstrated its full effect as a political organisation.

The final years: 1886-91

Despite the closeness of his association with the Liberals, Parnell remained the pre-eminent figure in Irish politics. In late 1886, however, further bad harvests revived the land issue. Evictions increased and the National League augmented what was to be termed the 'Plan of Campaign'. This form of resistance to landlordism was based on tenant collectives which offered reduced rents and, in the case of refusal, a boycott of the lands of those evicted. Inevitably, the Conservatives' answer was coercion and the Irish Secretary A.J. 'Bloody' Balfour came to epitomise the mis-rule, in Irish eyes, of his government. This time Parnell could count on Liberal support as he had not during the Land War. On his political platforms in Ireland, Parnell was joined by Liberal members who denounced the evils of the Conservative government. Such occasions demonstrated that the Irish leader was in greater control than he had been during the Land War: Parnell had reached the zenith of his popularity and respectability.

In response, in 1887, a campaign was launched against Parnell in an attempt to tie him to agrarian crime. The alleged evidence was a letter which he was supposed to have written about the Phoenix Park Murders: 'Though I regret the accident of Lord Frederick Cavendish's death, Burke got no more than his deserts.' *The Times* published the letter, which was later proved to be the forgery of a journalist, Richard Pigott. Parnell's exoneration further enhanced his already immense aura. During 1889 and 1890, he had been the 'uncrowned King of Ireland'. He was at his apogee; he was the apotheosis of Irish politics; he was even a guest at Hawarden, Gladstone's Flintshire estates.

Then in December 1889 Captain O'Shea, one of Parnell's supporters, made public the news that he was to be divorced: Parnell was named as co-respondent as he had conducted a liaison with Katharine O'Shea for almost a decade, during which time she bore his children. In December 1890, when the case came to court, Parnell found himself at the centre of a public scandal. Gladstone, his ally since 1885, was put under tremendous pressure to abandon the Irish leader. As the man who symbolised the moral values of his time, Gladstone cannot have found the decision difficult. In November 1890, he made public his belief that, while Parnell remained, Home Rule was unthinkable. Within two weeks the majority of the Irish Party took a similar position to Gladstone's: under Justin McCarthy, 43 anti-Parnellites broke away from the 27 who supported their old leader.

Parnell, in the face of this desertion but with his faith in himself unshaken, took his fight to the country. He was convinced, wrongly, that his Ireland would save him. The clergy were without equivocation determined that Parnell must go. Perhaps the leader underestimated the strength of such clerical influence in a religious country.

Although he spent much of his time touring the Irish countryside, canvassing support, where once he was a god he met dwindling crowds and some overt animosity. Desperate and ailing, Parnell nevertheless continued his travails and in early October he fell into a state of collapse from which he did not return. On 6 October 1891 Parnell died in the arms of his wife Katharine, the former Mrs O'Shea: he was 45.

Conclusion

During his last desperate campaign Parnell had reverted to the language of Fenianism which, to him, had always sounded hollow. He appealed to Ireland's marginal people — the poorest of the peasants — but failed. Irish politics had moved on from the days of the 1860s and 1870s, ironically, partly as a consequence of Parnell's work. In 1885–86, when Parnell tied himself to the Liberals, he had surrendered Irish political independence. Gladstone's subsequent withdrawal of support, together with the hostility of the Catholic clergy, had been decisive. In the early 1880s, it was Gladstone who had to accommodate Parnell, but by 1890, the Liberal leader represented the clearest hope for Home Rule. Until 1894 Gladstone would go on to fight vainly for the cause.

Parnell's achievements in negotiating with Gladstone, in modernising his party and in capturing the hearts and minds of his people, do not fully explain the myth of the man. Nor does the drama of a romance that scandalised conventional morality; even though this seems to be what most of posterity remembers of Parnell. Like most heroes he died young, and this too helps to explain his deification. Parnell is also remembered because of the political vacuum that is traditionally believed to have followed his fall. Parnell was in many ways an authoritarian figure. In December 1890 Parnell seemed to believe in his own legend and that he could carry the fight single-handed; he could not or would not see the changed political climate which he and Gladstone had enforced. As George Boyce has said: 'It was perhaps tragic, but appropriate, that, in 1886 Parnell destroyed Parnellism, and in 1891 Parnellism destroyed Parnell.'

Further Reading

Beckett, J.C. *The Making of Modern Ireland* (Faber and Faber, 1966).
Boyce, D.G. *Nationalism in Ireland* (Routledge, 1982).
Boyce, D.G. and O'Day, A. (eds) *Parnell in Perspective* (Routledge, 1991).
Brady, L.W. *T.P. O'Connor and the Liverpool Irish* (Swift, 1983).
Foster, R.F. *Charles Stewart Parnell: The Man and His Family* (Harvester, 1976).
Foster, R.F. *Modern Ireland 1600–1972* (Penguin, 1989).
Lyons, F.S.L. *Ireland Since the Famine* (Fontana, 1973).

Lyons, F.S.L. *Charles Stewart Parnell* (Collins, 1977).
O'Brien, C.C. *Parnell and his Party* (Open University Press).
O'Day, A. *The English Face of Irish Nationalism: Parnellite Involvement in British Politics 1880–86* (Gill and Macmillan, 1977).

Donald MacRaild teaches History at the University of Sunderland.

Christopher Collins
Britain and Ireland 1880–1921

The Irish Treaty of December 1921 sealed the partition of Ireland. The forces that shaped this settlement and brought about partition remain controversial.

The Irish question once occupied an undisputed place at the centre of British political life. For much of the period between 1880 and 1921 it provided the *raison d'être* for British party conflict. The two major British parties pursued profoundly opposed Irish policies, and each party operated in close alliance with Irish partners, themselves locked in deep and seemingly insoluble dispute as to the future of their country. Few features of the British political scene seemed to possess anything like the permanence of the Irish question, and very few also had its bitterness and violence.

And yet by 1921 it was common in Britain to suppose that the Irish problem had been solved. Party politics had moved on to new issues. Even the lingering problem of Ulster seemed marginal, and events in the province since 1968 — however tragic — have confirmed the judgement from the perspective of British party politics. The British parties do not fight about Northern Ireland. The British electorate is not deeply moved by the issue one way or another.

So how was the trick performed? How, and why, was the Irish problem 'solved', or at least removed from the political frontline? To answer that question obviously demands a definition of the problem. One has to begin long before 1880 to provide the necessary background.

Origins of the Irish question

From the twelfth until the twentieth century, Ireland was an element within the British state. Its constitutional position developed from that of a colony to one of full theoretical equality with the other components of the United Kingdom, secured by the Act of Union in 1800. The nature of the Anglo-Irish conflict changed considerably in the course of eight centuries. It began as a conflict between a colony and its imperial masters. During the sixteenth and seventeenth centuries religious differences came to overlie the earlier and persisting colonial struggle: the Reformation brought about the creation of a Protestant state in Britain, while the bulk of the Irish population remained Catholic. Religion became the touchstone of political allegiance. Catholicism was tainted with disloyalty to the state. Within Ireland British power was used to establish the ascendancy of a small Protestant minority, holding a monopoly of land and political power (then almost inseparable concepts), with Catholics dispossessed violently of both.

Finally, in the course of the eighteenth and nineteenth centuries the rise of nationalism in Europe superimposed a third layer of conflict, or refashioned the other two: a largely Catholic Irish nationalism emerged, aiming at the creation of an independent Irish state, or at the very least a greater measure of autonomy for Ireland within the United Kingdom. The Protestant Irish were largely alienated from the nationalist movement and became strong defenders of the Union. Their continued dominance in Ireland was perceived to rest on their maintaining the closest possible links with Britain and, in turn, the association with Protestant ascendancy damned the Union on the Catholic side.

Within Ireland as a whole, Protestants always formed the minority. However, in the north-eastern province of Ireland — Ulster — Britain successfully fostered Protestant emigration from the mainland during the seventeenth century, mainly from Scotland. Ulster thereby acquired, and has retained, a religious and political identity quite distinct from that of the rest of Ireland. Opposition to the twin phenomena of Catholicism and Irish Nationalism was strongest and most militant there, and Ulster Protestants acquired a traditional ethic of political self-reliance and a willingness to resort to force. In Ulster alone, Protestantism and Unionism achieved wide support in the community, unlike the south and west of Ireland where they were the preserve of the landed and professional élite.

The singularity of Ulster ultimately came to play a central part in the whole Irish dispute, but at the beginning of the period 1880–1921 the crucial significance of Ulster was not altogether apparent, even to its partisans. The emergence of 'the Ulster question' was a slow counterpoint to the development of the more familiar Irish question, 1880–1921.

Class politics in Britain

Much of the modern literature on the Irish question has been concerned with its impact on British politics, and has been written from a British Westminster perspective. A consensus has emerged among British Westminster historians about the *British* aspect of the Irish question in the period 1880–1921: broadly, the view is that the Irish question was of declining importance in British politics after the mid-1880s as class issues became the dominant currency of British political dispute. Certainly, with respect to the crucial Edwardian period, it is a common judgement that the Irish question was in decline as an issue between the British parties, largely because the electorate was polarising on class lines and becoming deaf to issues that did not fit in to the bread and butter framework.

Therefore, how far Ireland really *mattered* to Britain is one of the most important issues we need to consider in assessing the events of 1880–1921. If Ireland *did not* really matter to Britain, then why did the British parties argue so bitterly about it? One answer has been suggested by a number of prominent British historians, in a variety of forms: simply, they suggest, the British parties argued about Ireland because it suited them, for their own reasons, to do so. In particular, it is commonly assumed that the Conservative Party derived a significant party advantage from its opposition to Irish Nationalism and to nationalist demands for a repeal of the Union and the creation of an Irish Parliament in Dublin ('Home Rule'). The most influential study of the major Irish crisis of 1885–86 took this line: Alistair Cooke and John Vincent's *The Governing Passion* (1974). Cooke and Vincent focused on the moment when Gladstone led the Liberal conversion to Home Rule, splitting his party and driving its right wing — and the most prominent figure on its left — into the arms of the Tories. For Cooke and Vincent, both British parties and their leaders were irredeemably opportunist about the Irish question, caring little for what actually happened in Ireland, except in so far as it enabled them to improve their positions at Westminster. Subsequent historians have hesitated to take so unequivocal a line, but the notion that the Tories needed the Irish question for domestic British reasons is very strongly rooted in the literature.

Work on the political crises of 1909–11 has repeated the claim. The best history of the House of Lords' rejection of the Lloyd George budget in 1909 (Bruce Murray's *The People's Budget*, 1979) argued that the Conservatives were motivated partly by a desire to drive the Liberal government into dependence on Irish votes and so force Home Rule on to the immediate political agenda, to their own party advantage.

Does this line of argument make sense? Certainly, it does no justice to the depth and intensity of Tory feeling about Ireland to treat Unionism as a purely opportunist position. Few historians would claim that. And yet, the milder claim that the Tories made the best electoral use they could of their real commitment to the Union exposes clearly that Irish politics did matter to the British parties. Research on British Liberalism has confirmed that impression. Patricia Jalland's study *The Liberals and Ireland: the Ulster Question in British Politics to 1914* (1980) concluded that Liberal commitment to Home Rule was genuine, and not — as Tories often claimed — the straightforward product of Liberal dependence on Irish Nationalist votes.

The truth is that the Irish question mattered to the British parties for historical, ideological, economic and military reasons. It was an issue that touched deeply the existence and well-being of the British state. It was as important, and as appropriate and natural an occasion for party differences in Britain as class or any other issue. For much of the 1880s, during 1912–14 and again in 1920–21, Ireland was the dominant political issue at Westminster. Obviously, at times, class and other types of problem pushed Ireland off the immediate political agenda. But even at the height of the First World War Irish issues remained important enough to require the detailed political involvement of busy London politicians. On the first day of the Somme, 1 July 1916, commentators were predicting the break-up of the British government over Ireland. The economic, military and political significance of Ireland was sufficient to force it to the attention of Westminster, and the rise of class politics — a shift in the political culture of the mainland — did not displace Ireland from the political frontline in Britain.

The origins of partition

If we believe that Ireland genuinely mattered to the British, then the nature of the long Irish crisis that led to the settlement of 1921 becomes a lot clearer. In particular, it makes it possible to get a clearer view of perhaps the central question now asked about the settlement: why was Ireland partitioned? There have been two principal theories about partition. They underlie the present-day conflict in Northern Ireland, and for that reason the difference between them is anything but academic.

The first theory might be described as the **Old Nationalist or Republican** theory. Its principal exponents at present are Provisional Sinn Fein and the IRA. On this view, British interests were dominant in the decision to partition Ireland. Far from being indifferent to Irish affairs, the British were anxious to keep a foothold on Irish soil, perhaps for strategic reasons, or out of a less tangible concern with Imperial prestige. Although the British claimed that Protestant-Catholic divisions made a united Ireland impossible, the truth (old nationalists would say) is that the British fostered and exaggerated those divisions to give them a pretext for partition. Partition then was something *artificial*, *synthetic*, imposed on Ireland for their own reasons.

The second theory one might describe as **New Nationalist** or **Mainstream British** theory. This is the view dominant now in the Irish Republic and also in Britain. On this theory, partition was overwhelmingly the result of Protestant-Catholic divisions within Ireland. The British did not impose partition so much as acknowledge the aggressive determination of Ulster Protestants never to submit to Catholic rule. On this view, effectively, the Protestants were able to secure self-determination for themselves by the formation of a powerful resistance movement to Home Rule in 1911–12. Irish nationalists did little to encourage Protestants to join the movement for Home Rule or to become a part of the Irish state after 1921, and so perhaps they must share part of the responsibility for partition. But it is clear whatever one thinks of this last point, that on the new nationalist/mainsteam British theory, the Irish partitioned Ireland, rather than the British.

It should be clear immediately how these two theories fit into the argument about class politics in Britain. Broadly, supporters of the new nationalist/mainstream British position on partition tend to be those who believe in the fading of Irish issues in Britain as class politics emerged. They see Irish interests and concerns shaping the settlement far more than British. The old nationalism fits badly with such a view, for obvious reasons. For old nationalists, British interests were dominant in the settlement.

The pre-war crisis 1911-14

Historical analysis can go some way towards assessing these competing theories of partition, though it is plain that both old and new nationalists have deep moral and emotional commitments to their respective positions, which no academic account could expect to shift. It makes sense to start with an examination of the pre-war Irish crisis of 1911–14, in which partition first emerged as a serious possibility, and which also marked the end of the straightforward role of Ireland as a dividing line between the parties. After the outbreak of war and the formation of a coalition government in 1915, Irish issues remained significant and controversial, but the two major parties co-operated on Irish questions, and the divisions Ireland provoked were intra-rather than inter-party.

Partition was not an issue at the outset of the crisis. The Liberal government — dependent after 1910 on Irish votes in the Commons — introduced a Home Rule bill in 1912 in the face of bitter Unionist opposition. Unionists argued that the government had no electoral mandate for the measure, that the issue should be put before the electorate — either at a general election or by referendum — and that the case against Home Rule remained as strong as ever, for British and Irish reasons. Ulster's resistance to Home Rule was thus only one among many Unionist arguments.

However, in the course of the two years which the Home Rule measure required to pass into law under the new Parliament Act of 1911, Ulster became more and more prominent in Tory rhetoric. This was partly because Conservatives in Britain believed it to be their strongest argument electorally, but also because Ulster's willingness to resist Home Rule quickly led to the formation of a military movement in the province, threatening the authority of Parliament. Many Tories privately were disturbed at Ulster's extremism, but in public the party leadership solidly backed everything that Ulster did.

By 1913–14 both Unionists and Liberals in Britain were anxious for a settlement. A nationalist military movement developed, explicitly emulating Ulster and further threatening the foundation of the British state in Ireland. Compromise seemed the only alternative to civil war. But the only conceivable basis for a compromise was partition. Reluctantly, Ulster was prepared to accept this, though its original hope had been to kill Home Rule altogether. Many Tories disliked partition, but feared to oppose it in the absence of alternatives.

It might seem at first sight that these events strengthen the new nationalist position on partition. Irish realities dictated the British conversion to partition: the fear of armed conflict between the two unofficial military forces in Ireland. Yet it is important to see that Ulster itself was heavily dependent on the support of the British Tories to establish its position. Its leaders were desperate to avoid a military conflict, which they expected to lose. They needed a settlement by compromise at Westminster. And without the authority and power of Westminster — its troops, its funds and credit — the creation of a separate political unit in Northern Ireland would have been inconceivable. Old nationalist historians have made this very clear, notably John McColgan in *British Policy and Ireland Administration 1920–22* (1983) and Michael Farrell in *Arming the Protestants* (1983).

Thus the British *did* partition Ireland. To that degree, there is truth in the old nationalism. The Ulster Unionists could not have done it alone. At the same time, events in Ireland forced the British parties into accepting partition, and their motives do not appear to have been colonialist/imperialist, as old nationalists would claim. The new nationalism also has some value in explaining the settlement.

War and its aftermath 1914–21

By the outbreak of war in 1914 partition had come to seem inevitable to many in Britain and Ireland. However, much else was obscure. What kind of settlement would be made for the rest of Ireland?

The war did much to resolve that issue. At the outbreak of the conflict Home Rule had been on the verge of passing into law. The Liberal government decided to pass it into law, but suspend its operation for the duration. As a result, the Irish Nationalist Party was left vulnerable to attack by critics on the nationalist side, many of whom were strongly placed in the nationalist military movement — over which the nationalist party had incomplete control. At Easter 1916 a faction seized the centre of Dublin and held it for a week. They had no hope of military victory, but intended to make a gesture that would radicalise nationalist opinion and create pressure for an independent Irish

Republic. They succeeded. At the general election of 1918 the Irish Nationalist Party suffered virtual annihilation and the radical movement's MPs under the umbrella of Sinn Fein seceded from Westminster and formed the first Dail (independent Irish Parliament) in Dublin.

Between 1919 and 1921 the final scenes were played. British rule in the south and west gradually disintegrated as the Dail's military wing (the IRA) mounted an increasingly successful guerrilla campaign. The Dail itself successfully usurped many of the functions of the British state, establishing its own courts and raising revenue. British countermeasures grew ever more drastic and further alienated nationalist opinion.

Partition came in 1920, but was not secure until the Irish Treaty of December 1921 that ended the war in the south. The Lloyd George government skilfully negotiated with Sinn Fein to secure a settlement very favourable from the British angle: Ireland was to have Dominion status, with provision for British military bases to be retained at strategic ports. The nationalist demand for an end to partition was met by the proposal to establish a boundary commission to adjudicate on the north-south border, with the hint that its findings might render a separate Northern Ireland unviable — a fig leaf for the nationalists, which unsurprisingly came to nothing.

Conclusion

The settlement of 1921 neatly removed the Irish question from the British political agenda for almost 50 years. The forces that shaped the settlement and brought about partition remain controversial because the present dispute in Northern Ireland turns upon opposing theories on those questions. It is hard in fact to support without qualification either the new or the old nationalism. Both contribute a valuable perspective. It is difficult also to accept the strong claims made by many British historians about the primacy of class in Edwardian politics.

Christopher Collins is a research assistant on *The Thatcher Memoirs.*

PART II
Disraeli, Conservatism and Empire

The Liberals had descended into disarray before 1874. The difference then was that the Conservatives were better organised to capitalise on this. The National Union of Conservative and Constitutional Associations was set up to organise the new voters of 1867. This was followed by the Conservative Central Office in 1872. The same year saw Disraeli's Manchester and Crystal Palace speeches to the National Union. Much has been made of these, but one of the things that should stand out is the rarity with which Disraeli made such public pronouncements. Gladstone, in contrast, was by 1868 already an outdoor performer. He was to take this a stage further during his Midlothian campaign, virtually inventing the whistle stop tour with his impromptu speeches at every railway halt. These speeches were reported at length in the burgeoning local and national press. The platform, the press and photography were of growing importance as means of political communication from the 1870s which Gladstone proved more adept than most in exploiting. Indeed, he played a particular role in the development of the first. Lord Salisbury complained to the Queen in 1887, 'this duty of making political speeches is an aggravation of the labours of your Majesty's servants which we owe entirely to Mr Gladstone'.

Although some Tories, such as Lord Randolph Churchill, took to the platform readily enough, the vulgarities of the platform were not for Disraeli. His and Salisbury's approach to electoral politics was more traditional. The Liberals at the same time had other potential advantages. Of the 1,376 daily and weekly papers in circulation in 1880, most of them of recent vintage, 482 supported the Liberals and only 330 the Conservatives. If the Conservatives had the National Union, the Liberals had the National Liberal Federation founded in 1877.

The Party leadership, meanwhile, remained wedded to the principles of aristocratic government. Its social and electoral basis was, however, shifting. As Derby had already recognised in the 1860s, the middle classes were increasingly 'the strength of our party', a strength that was more fully realised after the redistribution of 1885. The Conservatives also picked up working class votes on a combination of patriotism and social reform. Much was made of the comments of Alexander Macdonald, elected in 1874 as one of the first working class MPs, in 1879 that, 'the Conservative party has done more for the working classes in five years than the Liberals have in fifty'. Gains in borough seats were, however, cancelled out in 1880 by losses in rural areas, as British agriculture was undercut by cheap imported grain and meat (made possible by the opening of the North American prairies and the introduction of refrigerated shipping) and, in 1885, by the enfranchisement of working class rural voters. It took the issue of Ireland after 1886 to at last secure a period of Conservative electoral domination.

Robert Blake
Disraeli:
Political Outsider

Robert Blake assesses Disraeli's political career and compares his achievements with those of Gladstone.

On any view Disraeli was one of the strangest figures to have reached No. 10 Downing Street during the Victorian age. He was the first 'outsider' to become Prime Minister. By this I mean that he was the first man who did not belong to the political élite. One has only to look at his predecessors and immediate successors to see what an exception he was, the son of a middle-class Jewish literary man, who had been educated at obscure schools and had not been to a university.

The Outsider

Wellington was a duke; Peel was the son of a millionaire and went to Harrow and Christ Church; the 14th Earl of Derby (Eton and Christ Church) was one of the great landowners of England. So was Disraeli's successor, the 3rd Marquess of Salisbury (also Eton and Christ Church) and he was followed by his nephew A.J. Balfour (Eton and Trinity College, Cambridge) who was a wealthy Scottish landowner. What was Disraeli doing in that *galère*?

Nor was the patrician dominance confined to the Tories. The leaders on the Whig Liberal side during Disraeli's political career were an earl, a viscount, a younger son of a duke and another viscount;[1] the only plain 'Mister' was Gladstone who was wealthy, educated at Eton and Christ Church and married into the aristocracy. When he retired he was succeeded by an earl.[2]

Disraeli's background and early political career

So Disraeli was an exception to the normal rules and was recognised as such by contemporaries as well as by posterity. He had been in his youth a dandy, a poseur and an extravagant spender. He had written colourful and slightly absurd novels until in 1844 he broke through with the first of his real successes, *Coningsby*, which is a brilliant conversation piece as readable today as when it first came out. But he had a millstone round his neck — the first novel he wrote, *Vivian Grey* (1826), which is avowedly autobiographical. It is an outrageous piece of youthful egotism and braggadoccio. When he became prominent in politics his enemies used it against him again and again. He would have liked to suppress it, and he amended the text. But it was as irrepressible as its author. He might try to laugh it off. He could not live it down. Disraeli, socially and politically an outsider, had formidable barriers to overcome, but he erected some of them himself. His family was not obscure and there was money there. He had the important asset that, though a person of Jewish ancestry, he was brought up as an Anglican. Had he been a Jew by religion as opposed to birth, he could not have entered Parliament until the late 1850s. 'It is really nonsense', wrote the Duke of Argyll in his *Autobiography and Memoirs* (1906), 'to talk of a man in his position as a mere "Jew Boy" who by the force of nothing except extraordinary genius attained to the leadership of a great political party. The only impediments in his way were not in any want of external advantages but his own often grotesque and unintelligible opinions'.[3]

The Duke overstated his case. There were real external disadvantages for Disraeli. Jews were not persecuted but they were not liked and few people made the distinction between race and religion. Nevertheless Disraeli, not only by his eccentric opinions but also by his extravagant and raffish mode of life, created obstacles for himself which he could have avoided. He shared his mistress, Lady Sykes, with the ex-Tory Lord Chancellor, Lord Lyndhurst, and brought them both to stay at his family's house, Bradenham in Buckinghamshire in 1834 — a scandal which was remembered in the neighbourhood for at least forty years. In the 1830s he was constantly on the verge of being arrested and imprisoned for debt.

Indeed, the parliamentary privilege which protected an MP from this disaster was one of his reasons for seeking to enter the House of Commons. And he gave a general impression of lack of political principles, beginning as a Radical and moving for opportunistic reasons to the Tory side until he was elected MP for Maidstone in 1837. His maiden speech was a disaster and he was howled down.

He moved to Shrewsbury in 1841 and, though he was successful, he had the embarrassment of seeing the town placarded with lists, mostly accurate, of his unpaid debts. The general election gave Peel the premiership and Disraeli wrote an almost abject begging letter for office. Peel politely declined. In 1846 at the height of the Corn Law crisis when he was attacking Peel, he denied that he had ever written such a letter. He was lucky that Peel, for whatever reason, did not read it out to the House either then or later. In the 1837 Parliament Disraeli made no great mark, and there was no reason whatever for Peel to give him even a minor office.

Young England

Disraeli became much better known during the 1841 Parliament. He was the leader of the curious coterie of romantic idealistic young Tories who were known as Young England. They received publicity and a mixture of fame and notoriety. Disraeli had by the end of 1845 made himself, through sheer hard work and practice, into one of the most effective parliamentary orators of the day and he was something of a thorn in the government's flesh. He was the principal figure among those Tories of whom it was said: 'Why are the Tories like walnuts? Because they are difficult to Peel.' He had also written the two novels by which he will always be best known as an author: *Coningsby* (May 1844) and *Sybil* (May 1845). The second of them contains a particularly acid attack on the Prime Minister. Disraeli was something of a celebrity. 'There's Mr Disraeli', Queen Victoria exclaimed to the Duchess of Buckingham at a grand party at Stowe early in 1845.

Nevertheless, few people would have predicted much of a future for him at the end of that year. He could not now go over to the other side. Yet he had effectively burned his boats with Peel. Moreover, there was a host of politicians who were younger than he yet well ahead in the Conservative hierarchy, the most conspicuous being Gladstone.

Repeal of the Corn Laws and the fall of Peel

The repeal of the Corn Laws transformed the situation. Repeal in itself did not do this. It was inevitable sooner or later given the climate of opinion in favour of free trade, and was widely expected. What was not expected was that Peel should be the instrument of change. It seemed far more likely that Russell and the Whigs would be when the Conservative Cabinet broke up in November 1845 and Peel resigned. And this would have happened if Russell had not had a last minute attack of cold feet and returned 'the poisoned chalice' to Peel in December. If he had not taken office Peel could have given quiet opposition support to the Whig measure and would have escaped the principal responsibility. In the event he had to take it upon himself. And this gave Disraeli his chance.

If their leader was to advocate as Prime Minister the abandonment of the Corn Laws, the Conservatives were certain to be bitterly divided. The agricultural 'interest' was the backbone of the Conservative Party and, in the 1841 election, Peel had given no hint that he would ever bring in a measure so apparently damaging to the majority of his supporters. Disraeli had for two or three years been a critic of Peel as a compromiser, an appeaser, a pragmatist and a mediocrity. The turning point in his political career was his scathing repetition of this theme, delivered on 22 January 1846 after Peel had announced his intention to repeal the Corn Laws — delivered in circumstances different from ever before. Hitherto Tory backbenchers had listened to him with amusement and pleasure as an attacker of a leader whom many regarded as slightly pompous and self-satisfied, but not as a serious threat to Tory ideas. On the Corn Law question, however, Disraeli was expressing with superb oratory and brilliant satire deep feelings of betrayal, which they could never have articulated themselves.

It was a solo performance uncoordinated with anyone else, but it was applauded to the echo and it at once put Disraeli on to a higher political plane. It also put him into contact with someone whose partnership was essential in the battle to defeat repeal and overthrow Peel. This was Lord George Bentinck, younger son of the Duke of Portland, nephew of Canning and a grandee of the Turf. He was a person of violent feelings and regarded Peel as a traitor. The gentlemen of Old England would follow him; they would applaud, but never follow at that time, a shady Jewish adventurer like Disraeli. Bentinck and Disraeli had never met before, but they became fast friends, despite their very different background. One must remember that Bentinck was very much the senior partner, and that Disraeli never claimed to be more than a sort of aide-de-camp, 'a friend who sate by Lord George Bentinck' in the House. The two partners could not block the repeal of the Corn Laws, but they could and did wreak vengeance on Peel who resigned in June on the defeat of his Irish Coercion Bill — brought down as the Duke of Wellington put it, by a 'blackguard combination'. The consequences of the turbulent events of January to June 1846 were to split the Conservative Party for a political generation – they were in office in a majority only once between 1846 and 1886 – but also to put Disraeli into the opposition front bench. In 1847 he became 'Knight of the Shire' for Buckinghamshire and, financed by the Bentincks, set himself up in the following year as a country gentleman with a landed estate at Hughenden Manor near High Wycombe. He had arrived.

His rise had been enormously helped by his marriage in 1838 to Mrs Wyndham-Lewis, widow of his colleague in the representation of Maidstone. She was twelve years older, slightly dotty in conversation, but fairly rich and devoted to Disraeli. She had a life interest in a house in London and capital bringing in £5,000 p.a. (which in modern terms has to be multiplied by at least forty). She salvaged his finances and, although very mean in day-to-day living, never stinted on entertainment in aid of Disraeli's political or social advancement.

The events of 1846 in effect produced a new political party. The opponents of Peel were a majority of the old Conservative Party and a complicated problem of nomenclature arose. There were those who favoured 'Country Party' or 'Protectionists'. The party of Bentinck and Disraeli also had to start anew with fresh funds, whips and organisation. ..

The leadership of Derby

It is only, however, in the House of Commons terms that one can speak of 'the party of Bentinck and Disraeli'. Towering over both of them was Lord Stanley, heir to the 13th Earl of Derby but created a peer during his father's lifetime. First as Lord Stanley and after 1851 as the 14th Earl of Derby, he was to be leader of the new Conservative Party for twenty-two years and Prime Minister three times (1852, 1858–59 and 1866–68). He was the only person of political weight who had resigned from Peel's cabinet over the repeal of the Corn Laws. He was an addict of the Turf, a classical scholar and translator, a great orator, a very clever if slightly indolent figure, and in every sense of the words a grandee or a magnifico; 'the cleverest eldest son for a hundred years' was one description of him. Bentinck died in 1848. After complicated compromises Disraeli was recognised by Stanley in 1851 as the party leader in the Commons, though not very enthusiastically. There had been a curious past episode in Disraeli's relationship with the Stanley family — allegations that he had introduced a younger brother to a gambling den (a 'hell' in nineteenth-century parlance) whose proprietor was one of Disraeli's creditors. The charge was not true. Disraeli's conduct appears to have been altruistic and honourable. Later Stanley recognised this, yet he was never entirely cordial, and Disraeli was not someone whom he found naturally congenial. But there was no question of Derby jettisoning Disraeli or of Disraeli challenging Derby, even though he lost five successive general elections.

Disraeli soldiered on through long years on the opposition front bench. From 1846 until 1874, when he at last became Prime Minister with a clear majority in the Commons, he was in office for only a little over 5 out of 28 years. His onslaughts on Peel had brought him to the top of his weakened party largely because almost all those ahead of him in the Conservative 'Establishment' had followed Peel into 'the wilderness', as the phrase goes. To quote the Duke of Argyll again, referring to Bentinck's sudden death in 1848 when apparently in the prime of life: 'By this strange event Disraeli was soon left absolutely alone, the only piece upon that side of politics that was above the level of a pawn … He was like a subaltern in a great battle where every superior officer was killed or wounded.'[4]

Disraeli had been lucky. He could not have calculated on this development, nor could he have foreseen the course of events which was to put him in the running for the top position. But he had the gift, so valuable in a successful political career, of seizing the unexpected opportunity and exploiting it. As he himself said: 'The opportune in a popular assembly has sometimes more success than the weightiest efforts of research and reason.'[5] He also had the gift of patience. He had to wait for nearly 22 years after the fall of Peel before he succeeded Derby as Prime Minister and leader of the Conservative Party, and then he was in office for only ten months before Gladstone won a crushing electoral victory in December 1868. It was another six years before he became Prime Minister with an effective majority. He was now an elderly widower, and something, though not all, of his zest for life had gone. 'Power! It has come to me too late', he was heard to mutter after his triumph at the Congress of Berlin in 1878. 'There were days when, on waking, I felt I could move dynasties and governments; but that has passed away.'[6]

During the period from 1846 to 1868 Disraeli was Chancellor of the Exchequer three times, but his spells in office were brief. He made a hash of his first budget in December 1852 and was destroyed by Gladstone. His second and third spells as Chancellor (1858–59 and 1866–68) were characterised by Gladstonian orthodoxy. Whatever subjects the two great men disputed about after 1852, finance was not one of them.

The key event in Disraeli's career was the 1867 Reform Act. Until then he was not regarded as a certain successor to Derby. His skill in manoeuvring through the Commons a Bill which enlarged the franchise far more than the Liberals wanted or the Conservatives originally intended, and keeping the initiative in the government's hands, was widely admired. It was admired all the more because the government was based on a minority in the House and yet was able to control the crucial question of the redistribution of seats. When Derby resigned through ill health early the following year he had no hesitation in recommending Queen Victoria to send for Disraeli, and she did.

Disraeli and Gladstone

It is from this point onwards that one can date the famous duel between Disraeli and Gladstone. For the first time they faced each other as leaders of their respective parties not simply in the House of Commons but in the country as a whole, for Russell like Derby had resigned on grounds of health and age. This direct personal confrontation on the floor of the House of Commons lasted until the end of 1874 when Gladstone resigned the Liberal leadership, temporarily as it turned out, and in August 1876 Disraeli moved into the House of Lords.

We are now in a different political world from that of the years between the first two reform acts. Palmerston had created a conservative/Liberal consensus which made it very difficult for the Conservative Party to obtain office. With his death the consensus dissolved, and party divisions became more clearly defined. There was still a large measure of agreement. Disraeli and Gladstone believed in government by an upper-class élite. 'I am an out and out inegalitarian', Gladstone once said, and he deplored the disappearance in Oxford of the nobleman's gown with its golden tassel — the 'tuft' which 'tuft-hunters' hunted. As for Disraeli, he had long ago dropped protection, and when agriculture really did slump in the last years of his second premiership he made no attempt to revive it. He believed as much as Gladstone did in low taxation, Treasury economy and minimal state intervention.

Where they did differ was on religious, imperial and foreign policy questions and also on constitutional reform as against social reform. In foreign and imperial policy especially, Disraeli inherited the mantle of Palmerston — *realpolitik*, the assertion of English interests, and the playing down of moral issues. Gladstone, on the other hand, was a believer in moral codes, the rule of international law, the cause of nations 'struggling rightly to be free'. The difference between moralism and *realpolitik* is strikingly shown in their divergent attitudes towards the Bulgarian atrocities. Disraeli regarded the Turkish brutality as an irritating impediment in his policy of preserving the integrity of the Ottoman Empire which he considered to be an important barrier against the expansion of Britain's enemy, Russia. Gladstone regarded the atrocities as a moral outrage to be condemned whatever Britain's material and strategic interests might be.

They differed too on empire. Gladstone in the 1840s had been enthusiastic for the development of the colonies. By 1868 he had ceased to feel like this and he had never taken any great interest in India. It was Disraeli who saw a vacancy here, just as he had seen the vacancy left by Palmerston in foreign policy. His imagination was captured by the whole imperial concept, and he was able to capture the imagination of others. To make the Conservatives the party of a strong national foreign policy of 'England first' and to make them also the party of empire were the two most lasting legacies that he left.

Despite their relatively marginal political differences, they disliked each other, as Lord Granville put it to Queen Victoria, 'more than is usual among public men'. He added: 'Lord Beaconsfield has the power of saying in two words that which drives a person of Mr Gladstone's peculiar temperament into a state of great excitement.' It is seldom in history that two party leaders have so deeply dichotomised politics. One can only explain it by one of those mysterious aspects of personal chemistry which are themselves inexplicable.

I was once asked who was the greater man — a meaningless question if you think about it. My answer on the spur of the moment was: 'Gladstone was the greater statesman, Disraeli the greater "character".' But there has never been anyone else like either of them. They will be remembered, analysed and discussed as long as British political history is a living subject. I hope this will be for a very long time.

Notes

(1) Grey, Melbourne, Lord John Russell, Palmerston.
(2) Rosebery.
(3) *Autobiography*, i. (John Murray, 1906), p.280.
(4) Ibid., p. 279.
(5) Disraeli, B. *Lord George Bentinck, A Political Biography* (Colburn, 1852) p.56.
(6) Quoted in Monypenny, W.F. and Buckle, G.E. *The Life of Benjamin Disraeli, Earl of Beaconsfield* (Murray, 1920) vol V, p.299.

Robert Blake is a distinguished historian whose books include biographies of Disraeli and Bonar Law and the standard one-volume history of the Conservative Party.

Bruce Coleman
Tory Democracy

*Bruce Coleman argues that such reality as existed in Tory Democracy was
largely the product of opportunistic Bismarckian calculations.*

Was the term 'Tory Democracy' warranted by the policy and practice
of Conservative politicians? Certainly the Conservative Party in the
nineteenth century did not positively want democracy. Its attitudes to
franchise extension in 1866–67 and 1884, and to the emergence of the
populist Home Rule Party in Ireland were negative and nervous. The
Second Reform Act in 1867 owed more to Tory ambitions to prolong
office, to split the Liberals and to forestall a Liberal measure than to
genuine desire for a borough household franchise. Derby's government did not extend the county franchise significantly or redistribute
many seats. But because Conservatives wished to win seats and form
majority governments, they could not afford to neglect the newly
established 'democracy'. 'Tory Democracy' was thus part of the somewhat reluctant, mixed and ambiguous response to the threat posed by
an enlarged electorate and the growing political muscle of the larger
towns. Even traditionalist Conservatives like Disraeli and Salisbury
feared that merely negative and confrontational responses to the new
forces in the political nation would drive them into the arms of the
Liberals and promote further radicalism. Prudent Tories should provide their own version of 'democratic' policies to prevent worse.
Models abroad — first Napoleon III and later Bismarck — suggested
the possibility of taming mass democracy for conservative purposes.

The aftermath of 1867

The 1868 general election showed that the 1867 reform had done the
Conservatives little good. Only in the urbanised North West had a
Tory tide run, as native 'Protestantism' reacted against the immigrant
Irish and Gladstone's proposed concessions to Irish Catholicism.
'Protestantism' would remain probably the most genuinely popular
element in Tory constituency politics. (By the mid-1880s Ulster
Unionism would reinforce this position.) But more would be needed
to topple Gladstone's Liberal government. The thrust of Disraeli's
Manchester and Crystal Palace speeches in 1872 was an attack on
Liberal government for weakness abroad, the betrayal of Palmerston's
legacy, and the proffering of social reform — 'elevate the condition of

the people' — as a Tory alternative to Liberal political reform. Yet this social mission, vague even in 1872, was being played down before the 1874 election, quiet times were promised at home after the 'harassment' of Liberal legislation, and the Conservative victory entailed no commitment to or mandate for a social programme.

The measures that followed had mixed origins. Some would probably have been passed by a Liberal government. But the Lancastrian R.A. Cross, Disraeli's unexpected Home Secretary, had enthusiasms beyond those of most Tories. His labour law reforms of 1875, particularly the legislation of peaceful picketing, were welcome to the trade unions who had some support from Conservative borough members anxious about their seats at the next election. They were opposed by almost the whole Cabinet until Disraeli, sensitive to the electoral consideration, backed Cross. Another Cross measure of 1875, the Artisans' Dwellings Act, facilitated slum clearance and the provision of working-class housing but still precluded borough authorities from providing the housing themselves. It remained only 'permissive' legislation, enabling but not requiring authorities to undertake improvements. The 1876 Merchant Shipping Act went further than the government had wanted originally; it was forced on them by the Liberal Samuel Plimsoll's agitation and by pressure from the ports. Backbench MPs for port constituencies pressed the government to conciliate the seamen's vote.

Most of these measures did not involve party confrontation. Measures that divided both Liberals and Conservatives and passed with support on both sides could hardly be depicted as essentially Tory in character. After 1876, with the Treasury strapped for money and ministers diverted to overseas affairs, social legislation dried up. In the 1880 election, which the Conservatives lost heavily, little was made of their social record, and there were few signs of popular gratitude. In 1877–78 a populist 'jingoism' had appeared, backing the government's firmness with Russia, and some Tories had readily played to it, but this mood too had faded by 1880. Now the Conservatives again found the post-Palmerston 'democracy' distinctly uncomfortable. In Ireland the dramatic advance of the Home Rulers showed how threatening popular politics could be.

The 1880s

The brief extravaganza of 'Tory Democracy' associated with the dramatic career of Lord Randolph Churchill hardly disturbed that picture. Restiveness within the party's National Union after 1880 reflected borough Tory resentment at their losses of seats and at their neglect by the leadership. It was exploited for the personal ambition of Churchill, a young man in a hurry and hostile to the party's staid co-leader, Northcote. Behind these rumblings there was, certainly, argument over the appropriate style of Tory politics in changing times. Churchill personified a style of demotic politics — 'the platform', great meetings, newspaper publicity and stage-managed political drama – which traditionalists distrusted as alien to both the constitution and Conservatism. How far it all represented any deep dispute over legislative policy is unclear; Churchill's career, ruthlessly ended by Salisbury, remains open to both conservative and radical interpretation of his intentions, though his overall strategy was almost certainly conservatively Bismarckian.

More significant were other developments of the 1880s: the 1883 Corrupt Practices Act which turned parties to new forms of political organisation and finance; the Liberals' 1884 Reform Act which extended household suffrage to the counties and so enfranchised more agricultural labourers; the 1885 Redistribution Act, with its smaller single-member constituencies which Conservatives hoped would bring them gains in the boroughs to counter Liberal gains in the democratised counties; and the split in the Liberal Party over Gladstone's Home Rule Bill in 1886, which brought about a Conservative government until 1892, sustained by the Liberal Unionists around Hartington and Chamberlain.

All these developments required new Conservative responses. In Ireland, now dominated by the ideologically democratic Home Rule Party, the government combined firm repression with Exchequer subsidised land transfer schemes, a Bismarckian combination of political order with social concession. The gains in borough seats which the Conservatives made in 1885 and 1886 also had ambiguous implications. The strengthened representation of borough Toryism integrated it better into the parliamentary party and so reduced its friction with the party leadership and organisation. The new seats were predominantly of the prosperous suburbs and so reduced Conservative dependence on working-class electorates (except still in 'Protestant' Lancashire) while increasing the influence of the low-spending preferences of middle-class ratepayers. Admittedly the increasingly numerous professional and businessmen MPs were not always unwilling to use legislation and central administration for purposes of better government and social improvement. Between 1886 and 1902 C.T. Ritchie, a London and Dundee businessman and MP for East London constituencies, was a notable legislator at the Local Government Board, the Board of Trade (where he promoted industrial conciliation) and the Home Office. Ritchie, never a platform politician like Churchill or Chamberlain, represented a soberly progressive style of government which offered the electorate a Conservative alternative to radicalism.

The Unionist alliance

Liberal Unionism also had a mixed impact. The shift of the most conservative elements of the Liberal Party, including many free-market ideologues, over into alliance with the Tories strengthened the non-interventionist tendencies within the party. G.J. Goschen, banker, city politician and Salisbury's Chancellor of the Exchequer 1887–92, personified this development. On the other hand the restless dynamism of Joseph Chamberlain, with a group of radicals, was harnessed to Unionist government, which he joined formally in 1895. Chamberlain pressed the Conservatives to deliver constructive reform. His panaceas included local government reform, free elementary education, compulsory industrial accident insurance and old age pensions. He had wrung county councils and free schooling out of Salisbury's government by 1892, but on the latter two issues he was thwarted by hostile interests within the Conservative Party and in 1895 he directed his energies into the less frustrating field of colonial policy. Whether despite or because of the Unionist alliance, which kept resistance to Home Rule its central purpose, the Conservative Party was becoming more suspicious of social reform enthusiasm.

Salisbury's party

The mainsprings of Conservative policy in the 1880s and 1890s remained little changed: resistance to Home Rule, the maintenance of law and order, the defence of the state churches and their interests, the upholding of property, not least landed property, together with a firm defence of British interests internationally. Even the populist strands in Tory thinking were concordant with traditional positions: for example, the assertion of 'Protestantism' and the leanings towards a circumspectly protectionist 'fair trade'. One new cause, the defence of the drink interest, combined plutocratic and popular elements. Another development, however, showed the limits of Conservative sympathy for working-class interests. By 1900 trade unionism, which had now grown significantly, was a political issue of a kind it had not been for Cross and Disraeli. The Conservatives had adopted a largely anti-trade union stance, leaving the Liberals (and soon the emergent Labour Party even more) as the protector of union interests. Halsbury, Conservative Lord Chancellor from 1885, appointed judges hostile to the legal position of trades unions. The Taff Vale (1901–2) and Osborne (1909) judgments would show the unions and political Toryism arrayed against each other as much in the law courts as in Parliament and in public controversy.

This largely suited Salisbury, Unionist premier 1885–86, 1886–92 and 1895–1902. Though not totally immune to reform causes — he had sympathised with much-publicised problems of lower-class housing 1882–83 — he generally identified with property rights, the free market, cheap government (except over the defence estimates) and with what survived of the aristocratic ascendancy. Willing to incorporate business interests — the 'villa Toryism' of the suburban plutocracy — into his defensive coalition of property, he remained fundamentally distrustful of democratic tendencies. His leadership featured the increasing use of the Tory-dominated House of Lords to block measures of Liberal governments passed by Commons majorities. Salisbury feared 'socialism' as much as the more familiar radicalism of the Liberal left and viewed certain social measures, particularly those financed from the pockets of the prosperous, as no bulwark against but rather a half-way house towards socialism.

Conclusion

Disraeli's period as leader thus saw little Conservative commitment to 'democracy' in either its political or social senses, only a variety of personal and tactical enthusiasms, often related to electoral considerations, to offset the party's traditionalism, vested interests and inertia. As politics were reshaped and policy alignments crystallised over the following decades, the Conservatives, though making sometimes vigorous responses to electoral reforms once achieved, largely opposed both further democratisation and social measures that smacked of wealth redistribution. Tories now played the political game by more democratic rules but mainly in order to stave off what pessimists feared would be the long-term consequences of democracy.

Further reading

Blake, R. *The Conservative Party from Peel to Churchill* (Eyre & Spottiswoode, 1970).

Coleman, B. *Conservatism and the Conservative Party in Nineteenth-Century Britain* (Edward Arnold, 1988).

Feuchtwanger, E.J. *Disraeli, Democracy and the Tory Party* (Clarendon Press, 1968).

Marsh, P.T. *The Discipline of Popular Government: Lord Salisbury's Domestic Statecraft 1881–1902* (Harvester Press, 1978).

Smith, P. *Disraelian Conservatism and Social Reform* (Routledge and Kegan Paul, 1967).

Bruce Coleman is Senior Lecturer in History at Exeter University.

Duncan Watts
'Juggler Joe':
Radical and Unionist

A Radical Liberal who later became an imperialist minister in a Tory Cabinet,
who contributed to splits in both Liberal and Conservative parties, but who
remained an advocate of radical change to the end of his career. Duncan Watts
tries to explain the enigma of Joseph Chamberlain.

Joseph Chamberlain (1836–1914) was one of the most dynamic and
colourful politicians of late-Victorian England. He had conspicuous
qualities, among them relentless energy and drive, and organisational
genius. Although people could admire his abilities and practical
achievements, his manner aroused too much antagonism. He was
viewed with suspicion by some, and heartily disliked by others who
denounced him as an opportunist. They saw him as a man without
abiding principles who was, in the words of Lloyd George, rather like
the 'contortionist at the local Pavilion'; hence the nickname sometimes
used by cartoonists, 'Juggler Joe'.

Character and relationships

He presented a chilling image, with his earnest, often gloomy facial
appearance, and sharp, incisive features. Generally, he was not a team-
player, so that his achievements were sometimes accomplished in
spite of others, rather than with their willing co-operation. He believed
that: 'on every committee of 13, there are 12 who go to the meeting
having given no thought to the subject... One goes, having made up
his mind... I always make it my business to be that one.' Beatrice
Potter, who had a relationship with him in the 1880s, later recorded her
impressions.[2] Her insights were acute, the more so as they were not
those of a political foe. She was fascinated by him, and commented on
his 'energy and personal magnetism, in a word, masculine force, to an
almost superlative degree'. She also found him very domineering, and
many who came into business or political contact with him would
have agreed that 'running alongside this genuine enthusiasm is a passionate desire to crush opposition to his will, a longing to feel his foot
on the necks of others'.

There was also reason to doubt his scruple, and in three episodes his
behaviour aroused suspicion. The first two were personal tragedies. In

the divorce case of Sir Charles Dilke, Chamberlain at times seemed to be recommending actions which secured the maximum adverse publicity for his friend and Radical ally. Many suspected that Chamberlain was keen to see Dilke become more embroiled in an episode which would almost certainly ruin his leadership prospects. After the appearance of the 'Pigott forgeries', documents which suggested that Parnell was implicated in the Phoenix Park murders of 1882, Chamberlain was actively involved in the attempt to discredit the Irish leader. He may have persuaded Captain O'Shea to name Parnell as corespondent in a divorce suit which led to Parnell's downfall. Chamberlain's sons certainly wondered about their father's role. Chamberlain's handling of the events surrounding the Jameson Raid also created grave doubts about his integrity.

Yet the picture is unfair if concentration on his methods and approach leads to a neglect of other qualities and of his practical achievements. He developed into a fine orator, possessing a clear voice which carried to the far corners of any room, and Speaker Peel observed that he was 'the best speaker in the House with one exception, and the best debater without exception'. His audiences, particularly those used to his performances in Birmingham Town Hall, knew every mannerism that he possessed, and they warmed to his every flash of wit. He was 'Brummagem Joe', their champion, and they remained loyal to him throughout the vicissitudes of a long career.

Background and early life

Born into a fairly prosperous manufacturing family, he was sent to Birmingham in 1854 to represent his father's interest in the family screwmaking business. Drive and a flair for organisation made him a great success, and as rivals were bought up or driven out of business he was on the way to building a fortune. A Unitarian by background, he quickly became involved in local religious life. Unitarians believed in the Civic Gospel, the idea that politics was a Christian mission; only through political action could living and working conditions be improved. Nonconformity and political dissent were closely linked, and he became caught up in mid-century Radicalism. He became active in the Birmingham Liberal Association, in which he was to be aided by an able political adviser, Francis Schnadhorst, in building up a formidable party machine.

They were very successful in exploiting the opportunities presented by the increase of Birmingham's parliamentary representation in the 1867 Reform Act. Using new techniques of electioneering, the Liberals captured all Birmingham's three seats in 1868. Opponents scented 'the Americanisation of politics', and denounced the Liberal Association as a 'caucus', literally, a meeting of wire-pullers.

Chamberlain favoured a national system of elementary education, compulsory, free and non-sectarian, and became the Chairman of the National Education League to campaign for this. When the Forster Bill was published in 1870, the NEL strongly resisted the compromise which allowed the religious schools to continue, and even renew their strength. Nonconformist opinion was behind him, and his reputation now spread beyond his local base. In 1873, the Liberal Association won the local council elections, and Chamberlain was selected as Mayor. He could afford to retire from business in the following year, for he had made a fortune of £120,000.

Mayor of Birmingham 1873-76

Birmingham was a manufacturing town (granted city status in 1889) which had grown too quickly because of the Industrial Revolution. It had some of the most appalling housing in the country, particularly in the squalid area known as The Minories, where disease was rife. For a shrewd businessman with a social conscience, here was ample opportunity to demonstrate his ability and his concern. He launched a crusade to improve the appearance and facilities of Birmingham, and to enable people to lead better and more wholesome lives.

His policy of Municipal Socialism, involving the takeover by the Corporation of the gas and water supplies, resulted in better amenities than those available when the undertakings were in private hands. He strongly believed that monopolies should be in the hands of representatives of the people, and not provided by speculators in search of profit. His most impressive contribution was the Town Improvement Scheme which involved a major programme of slum-clearance, and the construction of a new thoroughfare, Corporation Street. Critics were fearful of the costs of 'la rue Chamberlain', and saw his plans as an act of folly. *The Dart* carried a local refrain:

It has been a dear bargain, there can be no doubt
And we say it without hesitation
It's a drain on our means we could well be without
Is this boulevard of our Corporation.

Others noted that members of the Chamberlain family had bought up land and benefited from the improvement, and that there was little replacement housing for the working classes. This was only provided later, as an afterthought in the 1880s. There was some carping on the council, from colleagues as well as opponents. Chamberlain brushed aside objections with scant regard for the feelings of those who stood in his way.

He was not a modest man, but when he wrote of his achievements few could question the immensity of their scale:

I think I have almost completed my municipal programme and may sing 'Nunc Dimittis'. The town will be Parked, Paved, Assized, Marketed, Gas-and-Watered, and Improved, all as a result of three years' active work and with the general approval of the great bulk of the ratepayers.

His was not empty Radical rhetoric; he provided practical Radical action in a vigorous programme of reform which made Birmingham a model for others to follow. In the words of one American observer: 'Birmingham was the best-governed city in the world.'

His Radicalism

On his election to Parliament in 1876 Chamberlain had a chance to demonstrate his reforming credentials on the national scene. He was a coming man, and had a reputation as a formidable Radical, with republican sympathies. He had long despaired of the Liberal Party, describing it in 1873 as a 'gigantic sham', and he was particularly out of sympathy with Hartington's leadership of the party, for he regarded Whigs as little better than Tories. He enlisted Gladstone's backing for the establishment of a National Liberal Federation in 1877, and the new creation gave the Liberal Party a highly professional organisation whose value was demonstrated in the next election in 1880. Opponents saw it as another example of his wish to Americanise British politics, and the word 'caucus' surfaced again.

The new Prime Minister was Gladstone, back out of retirement. The Premier was reluctant to include Chamberlain in the government, but eventually gave him the Presidency of the Board of Trade. At a time when the Liberal Party was becoming more Radical, Gladstone surrounded himself with ministers who were out of sympathy with the changing mood.

Chamberlain's work at the Board of Trade was unspectacular. The topics provided little scope for his Radical zeal and, lacking ministerial support, he was unable to gain a high priority for any of his proposals. He involved himself fully in other aspects of government work, and in his attitudes to events in Egypt and the Sudan it was becoming apparent that he was an imperialist in the making. A strong champion of the franchise reform of 1884–85, he mocked the Peers who attempted to obstruct it. Lord Salisbury was particularly singled out as being representative 'of a class who toil not neither do they spin.'

Chamberlain put forward a series of proposals, and after the government fell he published the 'Radical Programme' in July 1885. It was dubbed the 'Unauthorised Programme', to distinguish it from the official platform of the leadership.

69

Chamberlain's priorities, as set out in 'The Radical Programme' in July 1885, included:

- Reform of the House of Lords
- Triennial Parliaments
- Payment of MPs
- Manhood suffrage
- National Councils for Scotland, Wales and Ireland
- Democratic local government for the counties
- Disestablishment for the State Church
- Graduated taxation
- Land reform to assist agricultural labourers
- Free elementary education

As an election drew near, the commitments were reduced in scope and scale, and he stressed the last three points, particularly the policy of land reform ('three acres and a cow'). His bellicose language frightened his former Whig colleagues, and even Gladstone noted that 'Chamberlain's socialism repels me.'

Ireland

Chamberlain joined the third Gladstone Administration of 1886, and promised to give an 'unprejudiced consideration' to any bill on Ireland. However, he was particularly disappointed with the position he was given, the Presidency of the Local Government Board; he had wanted the Colonial Office. Chamberlain had shown an interest in Irish problems, and wished to tackle Irish grievances. He had put forward a scheme for an Irish Board to deal with local matters, and had developed this into a plan for legislatures for England, Scotland, Wales and Ireland, known as 'National Councils'. He had never supported Home Rule, and when he saw the contents of the bill he resigned to lead the attack upon it. His opposition was fatal to Gladstone's chances, and the measure failed to pass through the House of Commons by 30 votes.

The sticking-point in his opposition to Home Rule was the absence of any Irish representation at Westminster. He claimed that Gladstone's proposals were 'tantamount to a proposal for separation'. He believed that Home Rule would lead to independence, though the proposals were designed to prevent that possibility. The Irish were to be given an Irish Parliament, but key reserved powers in the areas of defence, foreign relations, trade and the coinage were to remain at Westminster. There was not a vast difference between Gladstone's proposals and his own, and he confusingly referred to his National Councils scheme as 'Home-Rule-All-Round'. He was insistent, however, that the 1886 Bill was not consistent with the preservation of a

United Kingdom, whereas his own system of government would have been.

Chamberlain was undoubtedly ambitious and some see his opposition to Gladstone as a bid for the leadership. If Home Rule was defeated, and Gladstone ousted, then as the second-most important member of the party his chances of achieving the highest position were good. He also clearly resented the treatment which he had received from Gladstone whose behaviour to Chamberlain had, at times, been less than generous. He had failed to advance his career when opportunities arose, and had never shown the consideration to which Chamberlain felt he was entitled. Ultimately, Gladstone did not much like him, for he always preferred people who had a certain social and academic stamp about them; he had also been caused much embarrassment and difficulty by Chamberlain's past behaviour. Principle, ambition and personal pique may all have played some part in Chamberlain's opposition to Home Rule. What is more certain is that the break with the Liberals over this issue was the pivotal point in his career. From now on he was increasingly to find himself on the other side of the political fence, for on what he regarded as the key issue he was at one with the Conservatives in defending the unity of the United Kingdom. He soon began to call himself a Unionist.

In 1893, he was active in the opposition to the second Home Rule Bill. His attacks were devastating, and the clash between him and Gladstone was as dramatic as it had been seven years earlier. This time, it was the House of Lords which blocked the measure, and Chamberlain was quick to defend the Second Chamber. He believed that on this issue it was representative of public opinion. The audacious Radical thus increasingly found himself working with the Conservatives whom he had once so despised. How could this happen?

Party lines were not, in those days, so tightly drawn. It was not as though he was really at home in the Liberal Party, and he had found it easy to cooperate with the Disraeli government over the Town Improvement Scheme. He noted that: 'In social questions, the Conservatives have always been more progressive than the Liberals.' Many of his social contacts were increasingly with the Conservatives, though he still sat on the Liberal side of the House until 1895. Increasingly, he had come to admire the lifestyle and comforts of his former opponents, and though he and Lord Salisbury viewed each other with deep distrust, a closer relationship developed. In 1895 he joined the Conservative and Liberal Unionist Government.

Imperialism

This time, he had the position which Gladstone had refused him back in 1886: he became the Colonial Secretary, though a more prestigious office was available to him. At the peak of his career, he tackled his new task with zest. He believed that the consolidation and expansion of the empire offered an escape route from the chronic trade depression of the late nineteenth century. He also put forward the contemporary doctrine of Britain as the 'trustee of civilisation'. He felt that Britain had a duty to spread the blessings of the British way of life, for to him the Anglo-Saxons were a 'chosen people' possessing virtues denied to other races.

Plans to bring about some scheme of Imperial federation failed to materialise, but he was instrumental in bringing about the establishment of the Commonwealth of Australia. In Africa and the West Indies, he practised his ideas on colonial reform. The study of tropical agriculture and medicine was encouraged, and his enquiry into economic conditions in the West Indies resulted in improved communications between the islands and a diversification of their economies. Above all, his stewardship of the Colonial Office was dominated by events in South Africa, where relations between the British government and the Transvaal were rapidly to deteriorate. The settlers, or 'Uitlanders', in the Transvaal felt aggrieved by the treatment they received from the Kruger regime. Chamberlain took up their grievances, which became the key issue in his dealings with the Republic.

Chamberlain's conduct of affairs provided opponents with plenty of ammunition, and he was accused of complicity in the Jameson Raid, an unsuccessful invasion of the Transvaal intended to overthrow the government there. He was cleared of any responsibility by a Select Committee of the House of Commons, but historians have generally been much more critical of his role. He almost certainly knew of the planned invasion, and hoped it would succeed; when it did not, he disclaimed responsibility. As a skilful political operator, Chamberlain escaped from his embarrassment with remarkable effrontery, but the episode was highly damaging in relations with the Boers, who became intensely suspicious of British policy.

As momentum for war developed in the next few years, he played for high stakes, and his anti-Boer stance undermined the chances of a settlement. He hoped that the Boers would back down from a military solution, but in October 1899, war began. To his critics, this was 'Joe's War', and Lloyd George condemned the confrontation as 'senseless and unnecessary'. Lloyd George also made a sharp observation about the way in which business interests had benefited from Chamberlain's policies; 'the more the empire expands, the more the Chamberlains contract'. Lloyd George was fortunate to escape with his life when he went to Birmingham Town Hall to deliver the message, and had to be smuggled away disguised as a policeman. When the war ended, Chamberlain recognised the need for reconstruction, and went to South Africa to proclaim reconciliation between the races: 'Henceforth, we are one nation under one flag. We have left the past behind.'

Tariff reform

Shortly before this visit, Salisbury resigned as Tory leader. This was the last time Chamberlain might have had a chance of the Premiership, but he was ill in bed at the time; he had anyway probably ceased to expect the call. He was, after all, not a member of the Conservative Party but a Liberal Unionist,[2] and Balfour, Salisbury's nephew, seemed the obvious and safer choice.

Chamberlain's last campaign was for a major revision of Britain's trading arrangements. He was aware of how much British businessmen were suffering because other countries were erecting tariff barriers against British goods, and saw the case for retaliatory action. He produced a plan for Imperial Preference which would help bind the colonies closer to Great Britain. This would have involved tariffs being placed on goods from outside the Empire, and no duties or lower ones on goods from within it. This posed a major challenge to the doctrine of Free Trade which still had widespread acceptance in Britain.

Chamberlain was never able to sell his idea to the working classes who were unconvinced by promises of better employment prospects; they feared more expensive bread. Chamberlain resigned from the government to publicise his views in the country, and Conservative disunity was seriously exposed, as some members backed Chamberlain, others Free Trade, whilst Balfour tried to hold the party together in some semblance of unity. Meanwhile, the Liberals were the beneficiaries, for they were able to rally support in defence of Free Trade and a cheaper loaf.

They handsomely won the 1906 election, but Chamberlain had the satisfaction of seeing Balfour and other senior Conservatives defeated, whilst he retained his own seat in Birmingham. His supporters were well represented on the Unionist side of the House, and he could have seized the leadership if he had so wished. He made no such attempt; a tired politician, he was reluctant to embark on a fight against his old colleagues. He had pushed himself hard in recent years, and soon he suffered the stroke which was to end his active career. He remained at Westminster, and lingered on for eight years until his death on the eve of the First World War.

Notes

(1) Beatrice Potter (later Webb), diary entry 1884, subsequently quoted in *My Apprenticeship* (Longman, 1946).
(2) The actual merger came in 1911 as part of a package of measures to improve the efficiency of Conservative Central Office.

Duncan Watts is editor, examiner and part-time tutor at the Politics Association. He is the author of *Joseph Chamberlain and the Challenge of Radicalism*.

Keith Surridge
Brits, Boers and Blacks:
The Boer War 1899–1902

Much new research has been conducted in recent years on the South African war of 1899–1902. Drawing on this, Keith Surridge analyses the causes of the war and its consequences for British politics and the British Empire, the Boers and the black population of South Africa.

The original white inhabitants of the Cape were of Dutch/ French/German descent and known collectively as Boers (farmers) and later as Afrikaners. Under Dutch rule they had known little administrative interference but, when Britain occupied the Cape in 1806, this situation changed. Many Boers decided therefore to move, or 'trek', northwards to escape the British. Eventually they established two semi-independent republics known as the Orange Free State (hereafter the OFS) and the South African Republic (known as the Transvaal to the British) on the borders of the two British colonies of the Cape and Natal. In 1877, Britain annexed the Transvaal to save it from bankruptcy and the Zulus, but in 1880–81, after the Zulus had been defeated, British control was overthrown (known as the First Anglo-Boer War). In 1884, the political map of South Africa was stabilised following the signing of the London Convention, when Britain recognised the internal independence of the Transvaal.

When gold was discovered on the Witwatersrand (Rand) the Transvaal became the richest state in the region, causing an influx of foreign (mostly British) entrepreneurs and labourers – known locally as Uitlanders (or Outsiders). The Boers denied these foreigners political rights because they felt threatened by the huge numbers that came to work in and around the mines. This attitude provoked a great deal of resentment within the Uitlander community, as they had done much to create the Transvaal's wealth. In December 1895, certain mine owners and South African businessmen, notably Cecil Rhodes, conspired to overthrow the regime in Pretoria by sending an armed force to provoke a rebellion in the mining districts around Johannesburg. The Jameson Raid, as it became known, failed dismally, but President Kruger believed the British government was behind the raid, and began to use the Transvaal's wealth to create a heavily armed state.

Joseph Chamberlain, the Colonial Secretary, and Alfred Milner, the

High Commissioner for South Africa, concluded that something ought to be done to help the Uitlanders in order to affirm British supremacy in the region. Milner, however, decided that only war and annexation would end the Transvaal problem. Chamberlain, and the rest of the Cabinet, while willing to be tough with Kruger, baulked at a war without adequate public support. But in 1899 negotiations to provide some political rights for the Uitlanders broke down as Kruger's concessions did not go far enough, and Milner allowed little room for manoeuvre. Surprisingly, on 11 October 1899, Kruger, in alliance with the OFS, declared war on the British first, and sent his 'commandos' into Natal and Cape Colony.

The Debate

The origins of the war have provided historians with much to debate. Some blamed certain individuals for starting the war: notably Milner and Chamberlain. Milner was seen as uncompromising, and determined to force war on the Transvaal; whereas Chamberlain's actions were explained as attempts to avenge the failure of the Jameson Raid, in which he was implicated. But it is the prominence of gold that continues to enliven historial debate. In 1900, J.A. Hobson first suggested that Britain waged war to benefit the gold mining industry. Since then his ideas have been elaborated by numerous scholars. They believe that owing to economic competition from rivals, Britain sought control of a major gold source and the expanding South African market produced by the proximity of the gold mining industry. Consequently Chamberlain and Milner were determined to protect Britain's vital economic interests by going to war, and to stamp British authority in the region. This was done in collaboration with the mine owners (Randlords) who benefited during the war when Milner created the conditions for an efficient and profitable industry. Moreover, some scholars believe the South African situation should not be viewed as the only example of economically generated imperialism. For them the Boer War should be seen as part of a British global strategy, backed by the capitalists, in which the use of force to assert or defend British interests was of paramount importance.

Critics of this approach explain there is no evidence of British politicians collaborating with mine owners. Similarities between British policy and Randlord aspirations were coincidental, not premeditated. The politicians could not gain any benefits from an alliance with the Randlords, as they could not influence the mining process directly to enrich the British economy. In fact, gold never entered into British considerations. Before the war there was no gold shortage undermining the British economy. Explanations concerning the origins of the war should be sought in a broader context, engaging political, economic and cultural aspects in both Britain and South Africa. This debate, however, shows no signs of diminishing and continues to stimulate Boer War historiography.[1]

Campaigns

The military campaigns started badly for the British: three major towns were besieged — Ladysmith, Kimberley and Mafeking — and in the space of five days (10–15 December) three British armies were defeated, including one under the British commander Sir Redvers Buller at Colenso. This gave Buller's political enemies, particularly Lord Lansdowne, the opportunity to replace him, and on 18 December 1899, he was superseded by his rival Lord Roberts who, with Lord Kitchener, was sent to recover the situation as troops were poured into South Africa. The white dominions – Canada, Australia, and New Zealand – sent 30,000 troops, and this display of loyalty did much to enhance their sense of national identity.

While Buller stayed in Natal and attempted to relieve Ladysmith, Roberts and Kitchener invaded the OFS from Cape Colony. In a swift campaign, Roberts compelled the Boers to lift the sieges of Kimberley and Mafeking and retreat. Bloemfontein was captured on 13 March 1900, followed by Johannesburg and Pretoria on 31 May and 5 June respectively. By September, both republics had been annexed to the British Empire. When the British reached Komati Poort, President Kruger had fled and the Boers were cut off from the outside world: the war seemed practically over.

Guerrilla war

Lord Roberts left Kitchener to finish the war, but Boer commandos proved elusive and capable of easily disrupting the vulnerable British lines of communication. Just before Roberts left, he inaugurated a policy of farm burning as a punishment, and to deny the commandos supplies he began rounding up civilians in the Transvaal and OFS. This 'concentration' policy was extended by Kitchener until over 230,000 white and black civilians were placed in 60 concentration camps. Some camps were badly sited or inefficiently run, and thousands began to die through lack of care. This provoked a scandal in Britain and forced the civil authorities to take over the administration of the camps. Before conditions improved, however, some 42,000 civilians (mostly children) had died.

The Boer leaders placed their hopes on generating a Boer uprising in Cape Colony, and a number of small commandos were sent there to elicit support. Although 10,000 Cape Boers joined them during the war, many were unarmed or useless. Even so, the commandos proved difficult to catch, and this caused a major rift between the civil and military authorities in the colony. Cape politicians accused the military of contravening civil rights, especially in administering martial law; while the soldiers thought the politicians obstructive and unhelpful.

In the annexed republics, Kitchener inaugurated a scheme whereby the area was divided by lines of blockhouses and barbed wire. Eventually this proved successful; but this system needed an enormous garrison to maintain it, in addition to the mounted columns chasing Boers. It also caused a rift between Kitchener and Milner, the two senior British officials. This was because Kitchener's policy was slow and he proved reluctant to allow Milner to begin the reconstruction of the Transvaal, as it would divert resources away from the military. Milner wanted to use the opportunity to begin creating a British state without worrying about Boer opinion, but he could not shift Kitchener, despite pleas to London for support. Instead he had to wait till after the war and run the risk of Boer hostility. For the Boers, life on commando became intolerable as they were denied supplies and found diminishing support. Many Boers joined the British, as National Scouts, and fought against their own people. In March 1902, Kitchener's strategy of relentless pursuit and devastation of the countryside paid off when the Boers opened negotiations.

Britain and the war

Ironically, the early defeats sparked off a wave of jingoistic feeling, which led to a rush to join up, or to create special units to serve in South Africa: the City Imperial Volunteers are perhaps the most famous of these. Popular enthusiasm muted those individuals and organisations who tried to speak out against the war. They were attacked and their meetings violently disrupted. The celebrations following the Relief of Mafeking marked the high point of popular fervour, but as the guerrilla war dragged on popular enthusiasm declined. The pro-Boers (as critics of the war were called) found they could speak freely and without hindrance; yet they were never that influential.

However, the government was lambasted for underestimating the power of Boers resistance. And, as the war progressed, the scandal of the concentration camps weakened the government's prestige still further. The army's poor display, coupled with an exaggerated appreciation of Boer prowess, led to generalised criticisms of the whole fabric of British political and cultural society. Known later as the National Efficiency movement, these critics expressed concern over the apparent inability of Britain's political system to gear itself for war. The poor health and education of recruits from the slums led to fears that Britain would be unable to defend its interests militarily, or compete economically. The Unionist government retained its majority in the 1900 'Khaki' general election before these concerns had set in. They were assisted not least by the fact that the Liberals were split by the war and without clear leadership. Campbell-Bannerman, the Liberal leader, made one notable intervention when he described Kitchener's policies as 'methods of barbarism', a description that still finds favour today.

War and the working class

Some debate has centred on whether the working classes were in favour of the war or not. Hobson thought they were, after being appalled by the Mafeking Night celebrations. Critics of this view say the working classes displayed little interest in the war, as opponents of the pro-Boers were often middle class, usually students or clerks. In fact the Labour movement was opposed to the war from the start, but was not vociferous in its opposition.

An alternative view suggests there was working-class support for the war. Schooling and music halls imbued workers with imperialistic and military ideas, and these were reinforced by heavy working-class membership of the armed forces. However, it is acknowledged that working-class nationalism was unique and was not expressed in any coherent way. Historians have shown that at one moment the working class would show hostility to their employers, but then cheer a military parade or passing royalty. Working-class nationalism may have been illogical, but it should not be dismissed. What is certain is that never before had a colonial war provoked such fierce argument and controversy.[2]

Black people and the war

Many contemporaries and historians believed the war to be a 'white-man's war'. Recent scholarship has now shown this conjecture to be false. Many black and coloured people did take part, and without them the British war machine would not have functioned. Initially, the British armed blacks to defend their own locations, but did not use them in any major military capacity except as transport workers. In Natal, many Asians, including Mahatma Gandhi, became stretcher bearers in order to demonstrate their loyalty.

As the guerrilla war developed, and Britain was obliged to maintain an army of over 250,000 men in South Africa, the need for black and coloured labour and scouts became paramount. However, the army's insatiable needs threatened to upset the social balance in Cape Colony, as this was where most of the black and coloured recruits came from. Paying far higher wages, the army needed men to drive transport, or act as auxiliaries to help administer martial law.

White farm owners – both British and Boer – were incensed by the shortage of labour and the vengeful attitude of the auxiliaries. Boer farmers were arrested on suspicion of treason or murder, and the use of black witnesses against them caused uproar. In all these matters the army showed a complete disregard for the opinions of local whites; they cared only that blacks and coloureds should keep the war machine functioning.

In retaliation, Boer commandos shot many blacks and coloureds for resisting them or just for being employed by the army. Maritz's destruction of the coloured community at Liliefontein in Cape Colony was one such episode. But the Boers did not have it all their own way. In the Transvaal, the Pedi and Kgatla denied the Boers access to valuable territory and supplies, and in Natal the Zulus defeated a Boer commando at Holkraans after continual provocation. Up to 100,000 blacks and coloureds joined the army in some capacity. While some joined for economic reasons, a major factor for enlistment was loyalty and the hope for a better future, politically and economically. It was these who were to be bitterly disappointed after the war.[3]

The Treaty of Vereeniging

In March 1902, the Boers contacted Kitchener to begin negotiations. Eventually, the British authorities allowed a large delegation of Boers to confer at Vereeniging to decide whether they wanted peace or not, and to elect representatives. After much argument, the peace party prevailed and asked for terms. Milner wanted unconditional surrender, to destroy any hope of Boer resistance to his plans; but Kitchener and the majority of the Cabinet opted for terms as the best solution. The British agreed to compensate the Boers for the destruction of their farms, and not to extend black political rights, once they accepted the annexation of their republics to the British Empire. On 31 May 1902, the Treaty of Vereeniging was signed. War weariness on both sides ensured a successful conclusion to the negotiations.

In all some 22,000 British soldiers died, mostly from disease. The Boers suffered 7,000 combat dead, to add to the 28,000 who died in the camps. It is probable that some 15,000 blacks died overall. The British thought the war would cost £10 million; instead it cost £250 million, after 450,000 men served in South Africa. Some 30,000 farms were destroyed and innumerable animals died from slaughter or neglect.

Aftermath

Milner hoped to fashion a new British South Africa from the wreckage, but his hopes proved illusory. The mining industry, unable to obtain cheap labour owing to the postwar boom, could not pay enough tax to finance Milner's schemes. Another consequence was the use of

Chinese indentured labour which the Liberals made so much of in the 1906 general election campaign. Unable to entice enough British immigrants, and with British subsidies ending in 1903, the South African economy slumped. In March 1905, Milner resigned.

Milner had also failed to exploit the wartime divisions in Boer society, which were quickly healed by the Boer leaders, notably Botha and Smuts. By showing a united political front the Boers eventually convinced the British of their peaceful intentions and their loyalty, as a means to achieving a political union in South Africa. Now that Boer governments were installed in three provinces, the Boer leadership felt the time was right to agree to a British proposal for union, and so consolidate their hold over all South Africa. Asquith's Liberal government (1908–15) saw political union as the best way to prevent detrimental economic competition amongst the four colonies, to safeguard imperial interests and, hopefully, those of the black, coloured and Asian populations. This had been the British aim since the 1870s and when the Boers proved receptive to the idea, Asquith's government quickly brought it to fruition. On 31 May 1910, exactly eight years after the war finished, the Union of South Africa was created. Many non-whites were fearful of this, but the Liberals, by keeping Bechuanaland, Basutoland and Swaziland out of the Union, and by preserving the Cape franchise, believed they had looked after non-white interests. They considered that British interference was likely to do more harm than good, and so relied on the good sense of white politicians: union, they hoped, would soften white attitudes towards the black majority. Some Boers were also dismayed by the Union and refused to accept the British connection; these dissidents later founded the National Party. They eventually took power after the Second World War and became the architects of apartheid.[4]

Notes

(1) Hobson, J.A. *The War in South Africa* (J. Nistet, 1900). For a recent survey of the historiography see Porter, A. N. 'The South African War: context and motive reconsidered', *Journal of African History*, No. 1 (1990).

(2) Hobson, J.A. *The Psychology of Jingoism* (Grant Richards, 1901).
Porter, B. *Critics of Empire* (Macmillan, 1968).
Price, *An Imperial War and the British Working Class* (Routledge and Kegan Paul, 1972).

(3) Warwick, P. *Black People and the South African War* (Cambridge University Press, 1980).
Nasson, W.R. *Abraham Esau's* War (Cambridge University Press, 1980).

(4) See Hyam, R. in Warwick, P. *The South African War* (Cambridge University Press, 1980).

Further reading

Pakenham, T. *The Boer War* (Weidenfeld and Nicolson, 1979).

Porter, A. N. *The Origins of the South African War* (Manchester University Press, 1980).

Warwick, P. (ed.) *The South African War* (Longman, 1980).

Keith Surridge is a postgraduate student at King's College, University of London.

PART III
Labour, New Liberals and the Descent to War

The Boer War initially compounded the Liberal disarray which bene-fited the Tories in 1895 and 1900. As the war wore on, however, it also underlined growing anxieties about British national performance. Economic growth slowed in the late nineteenth century whilst the per-ceived need for greater national expenditure on defence increased. This not only prompted naval building programmes but the constitu-tional innovation of the Defence Committee of the Cabinet, trans-formed into the Committee of Imperial Defence in the wake of the Boer War. At the same time the war compounded the growing anxiety about the need to improve social conditions. Increasing concern at the perceived ineffectiveness of the Poor Law in assisting the aged poor led to a series of schemes for old age pensions from the 1880s onwards. The revelations about the poor physical conditions of many volunteers during the war also cast the spotlight upon children's welfare.

The formula for meeting all these problems of foreign economic competition, and the needs to strengthen the empire and finance social reform was, according to Chamberlain, imperial preference. This idea, however, ran counter to the still quasi-religious veneration of free trade. Tariffs, moreover, would impact upon working class living standards much more than the Liberals' preferred option of raising direct taxes. They weighed heavily against the Tories in the election defeat of 1906. In the circumstances of the sharp trade downturn of 1908–9, a downturn which increased anxieties about economic compe-tition from Germany and encouraged the hysteria surrounding the naval race, they might have had more appeal. However, by then Lloyd George was in charge of the nation's finances, and the means sug-gested of paying for dreadnoughts and pensions was a very different mix of increases in income tax and death duties and the introduction of a land tax. Whether or not this was a calculated attempt to provoke the House of Lords, the nemesis of so much Liberal legislation over the period since the 1880s, it certainly succeeded. The result was a lengthy constitutional crisis culminating in the 1911 Parliament Act. This mea-sure, which reduced the Lords' power to block legislation passes by the Commons to two successive sessions, was resisted by Conservative peers on the grounds that it would enable the forcing through of controversial, and to them repugnant, legislation such as Irish Home Rule or disestablishment of the Welsh Church. In 1912–14 this is exactly what happened. The Conservatives, despite reorganisation in 1911–12 and a series of by-election gains which meant that by 1914 they were the largest party in the Commons, were unable to challenge the Liberal control of Parliament.

Nor were Labour. The new party was making progress in some local elections. The Liberals' dominance of the agenda, however, meant that there was little room for manoeuvre in Parliament. The Progressive Alliance forged by the Pact between Liberals and Labour, in 1903, certainly gave Labour the opportunity dramatically to increase its parliamentary base. After the initial influx of Labour MPs in 1906 it, however, worked to curtail further inroads. The trade unions were certainly dissuaded from putting up the money for more candidates against a dominant Liberal Party, especially if that risked letting the Tories in. Labour only ran 56 candidates in December 1910. The result was a loss of impetus and declining membership of groups groups such as the ILP. Thus, by 1914 Labour still remained confined to being largely a ginger group on the fringes of the still great Liberal Party.

Peter Catterall and Joyce Howson

New Unionism

Why did it take so long before general unions for unskilled workers began to appear, and what contribution did the 'New Unions' of 1888–91, often led as they were by committed socialists, make to the rise of a political Labour movement?

Although the right to form trade unions had been conceded by the repeal of the Combination Acts in 1824 and 1825, many groups of workers remained unorganised until towards the end of the nineteenth century. This situation only started to change in the 1870s and 1880s. Strike waves coinciding with trade upturns in 1871–73 and, particularly 1888–91, saw the formation of new unions amongst previously unorganised groups of workers.

There were, however, significant differences between these two strike waves. By the end of the 1870s many of the new unions formed at the start of the decade had already disappeared. The new creations of 1888–91 proved more robust. Trade union membership also rose. Membership affiliated to the Trades Union Congress (which had been founded in 1868) had levelled off at the end of the 1880s at about 500,000. It hit a peak of 1,470,000 in 1890, before levelling off around one million for the rest of the 1890s. Total union membership (including members of non-affiliated unions) rose to two million by the turn of the century.

The second difference was between the political attitudes of the leaders of each strike wave. The leaders of 1871–73 generally had Gladstonian allegiances, as did the first two trade unionists elected to Parliament in 1874. Indeed, Joseph Arch, who founded the National Agricultural Labourers' Union in 1872, later sat as a Liberal MP. In contrast, many of the leaders of the 'New Unions' of 1889–91 were socialists, and later sat as Labour MPs.

Craft and 'New Model Unions'

The membership of these 'New Unions' principally consisted of previously unorganised unskilled labourers. Organisation had instead started amongst craftsmen. In the middle ages such craftsmen, in order to control who worked at a trade, where they could sell their products and at what price, formed gilds, the forerunner of unions. This situation began to change with the coming of the Industrial Revolution.

Industrialisation into factories gradually replaced craftsmen in cottage industries with a system of masters and men. Common action by craftsmen was now liable to be seen by the law as a restraint of the liberty of the employers to trade, a view which was put on a statutory basis by the Combination Acts of 1799 and 1800, passed during the crisis of the wars against Revolutionary France. This was because the government feared that trade societies were being used as a front for seditious agitation.

What the law did approve was friendly societies, and these received explicit legislative encouragement from 1793 onwards. Under cover as friendly societies some trades were, however, able to build effective union organisation even before the Combination Acts were repealed in the 1820s.

Craft unions were found amongst traditional trades such as masonry, carpentry, printing and barrel-making. These craftsmen continued to work in small-scale workshops in towns and villages as before, but improved technology brought drastic changes to some other industries, notably engineering and cotton. The transition to large-scale factory production replaced old types of craftsmen, such as hand-loom weavers, and required new categories of skilled workers. The importance of these workers to their industries gave them, and their craftsmen fellows, considerable bargaining power. This affected the pattern of development of unionisation in these new trades. There were some distinctions between the craft unions and the 'New Model Unions', of which the Amalgamated Society of Engineers, founded in 1851, was the archetype. Although in reality mainly confined to the industrial north of England, they were combinations of local unions (hence amalgamated society) into a nominally national structure. Otherwise many characteristics of the craft unions remained. It was in the interest of skilled workers to restrict entry to their trade, so as to restrict members and keep their wage levels up. Particular attention was paid to controlling apprenticeships, the initiation to the mysteries of the craft. In the cotton industry the spinners even paid the piecers, the apprentice spinners who worked with and for them.

The result was that unionisation in complex industries like cotton was vertical, not horizontal. The workers in the different sections of the industry, the spinners, the weavers, the card-room workers and so on, all had their own wage rates, their own conditions, their own skills and their own union.

There were attempts in the 1830s to create more grandiose structures, of which the most celebrated was the Grand National Consolidated Trade Union. At the same time William Benbow launched his idea of a 'national holiday' (ie general strike). These were the first signs of the idea of unions and industrial action to advance not just the cause of particular groups of workers but to effect social

change. This kind of language, and the idea of a national strike to win
social and economic gains very much anticipated the syndicalism
taken up by some unionists and Labour politicians during the
Edwardian period. Born to defend local unions in the context of an
employers' attack the GNCTU, however, proved to be a victim of the
circumstances of its nativity. Most of its short life was spent fighting
and losing costly disputes with inadequate financial backing. Within a
few months, in May 1834, it had all but collapsed.

An aristocracy of labour

The behaviour of the craft and skilled unions has, in contrast, often
been characterised as timid. Their unions were anathematised by John
Burns, then a socialist firebrand member of the ASE and later one of
the 'New Union' organisers of the London Dock Strike of 1889, as no
more than glorified friendly societies. Historians in the 1960s, seeking
a reason for the apparent decline in working-class activism between
the decline of Chartism and the appearance of small socialist groups in
the 1880s, criticised their 'aristocracy of labour'. They saw them as
besotted with bourgeois pretensions and trying to put as much
social distance as possible between themselves and the rest of the
working class.

The 'New Model Unions' certainly were at pains to emphasise their
sobriety and respectability. The ASE's evidence to the Royal
Commission on trade unions in the 1860s included the assurance that
strikes were the last thing they would want to encourage. Such assur-
ances helped to defuse middle-class criticism of unions, and to ensure
the improvement of their legal position during the 1870s (and, it
should be noted, helped to prepare the ground for the 'New Unions').
They were, however, slightly misleading. The ASE was quite prepared
to do what the GNCTU had been formed to do and subsidise industrial
action by workers in other trades, only it enjoyed more success than
the GNCTU had done. Between 1854–67 it provided such subsidies on
no less than 179 occasions. It was not strikes as such that 'New Model
Unions' objected to, but unsuccessful ones.

Industrial action is expensive. Losing can be even more expensive.
Arch's agricultural union never recovered from the farmers' response
in 1874, and the union's lack of success meant members gradually fell
away, seeing no point in paying dues from their meagre wages
towards the upkeep of an organisation that had failed them. It eventually disbanded in 1896.

This and the experience of the GNCTU illustrates the importance of
sound finance to successful union organisation. 'New Model Unions'
were, therefore, unwilling to risk their funds and survival on fights
they could not win. They also had other responsibilities, besides

industrial relations. Burns was right, in so far as their function as friendly societies was important to them. This, in part, reflected the legislative framework in which they had developed. But it also reflected the wishes of their members. Friendly societies enjoyed widespread working-class support. Whilst no more than ten per cent of workers were unionised in 1888 the figure for friendly society membership is probably nearer to eighty per cent.

Organising the unskilled

Friendly society benefits, such as sick pay, unemployment benefit, medical care and burial funds, were expensive and required high union dues. Unskilled workers were unlikely to be able to pay these dues in full. There was, therefore, little incentive for the 'New Model Unions' to extend their benefits to these workers in the mid-nineteenth century. Indeed, for many of these unions defending sectional interests, unskilled workers in the same industries posed a positive threat to their wage levels and living standards. This was particularly true as technological change began to reduce the skill levels required for some types of work towards the end of the century.

The other problem was the apparent difficulty of organising certain groups of workers. Few women were unionised outside the textile industries. Even in such trades, where they were worked in large numbers and strong unions existed, this was still often the case. This was partly because female participation in the work-force largely ended at marriage and 'the more benefit based the unions were, the less appeal they had for those whose careers might be interrupted'.[1]

The seasonality of employment meanwhile disrupted attempts to unionise agricultural labourers. Gasworkers were also affected by the seasons, many being laid off during the summer when demand fell. But the most famous example was that of the dockworkers. Whilst the London stevedores and watermen already had their own strong unions, many workers were employed on a casual basis, waiting in stands hired for the day. This reflected a labour surplus which made it easy for employers to resist unionisation. And even amongst casual dockworkers there were job specialists which militated against the formation of unions, divisions which were compounded by religious differences between Catholic and Protestant.

The growth of class conflict

The result was that by the 1880s, whilst unions had been consolidated in skilled trades, they only covered a fraction of all workers. The situation had, however, begun to change. There had been a steady drift from the land to the towns, filling new unskilled jobs in an increasingly mature industrialised economy. In the towns, meanwhile, an opposite movement was taking place. The middle classes moved out to the new suburbs, leaving behind working class concentrations. Meanwhile, although most firms remained family businesses, there were, from the 1850s, a growing number of limited liability companies owned not by local families but by shareholders. The introduction of limited liability also facilitated the rise of larger, more complex firms. These required a new army of managers to run them, a development which was trenchantly criticised by the Socialist League in 1885. J R Clynes, leader of the Labour Party from 1921 to 1922 was later to attribute the growth of socialism to this development[2]. The paternalistic firms of the past seemed to be disappearing.

> There was a day when the master took a paternal interest in 'his men' ... but today we have soulless companies and combines; the men have become machines for producing dividends for masters.[3]

At the same time this development was beginning to replace the fragmented sub-contracting economy that was clearly still in place in the mid-nineteenth century with larger-scale units. This reduced the social horizons of workers. In the mid-century it was possible to believe, by hard work and application, a man could become a master. The division, in many cases, was not that great. This was the aspirational culture in which Samuel Smiles' *Self-Help* (1859) could enjoy enormous popularity; in which those shining examples of self-made men, the great engineers, were lionised as emblematic figures of the Victorian age[4]; and of which Gladstonian Liberalism was the natural political expression. Its decline, and these other changes, disrupted the reciprocity of interest between masters and men which was supposed to exist under the principles of nineteenth century political economy.

It is possible to exaggerate the influence of this notion. As the secretary of the ASE, William Allan, told the Royal Commission of trade unions:

> Every day of the week I hear that the interests are identical. I scarcely see how that can be ... It is in their interest to get the labour at as low a rate as they possibly can, and it is ours to get as high a rate as possible.[5]

Nevertheless, it was generally accepted under classic political economy that the selling price of labour (ie wages) should rise and fall with the level of demand for an industry's products. This assumption was, however, being undermined by increasing adverse economic conditions. The period 1870–1913 was characterised by a series of sharp peaks and troughs in the rate of unemployment. Unemployment, supposed by the political economists to be no more than a purely temporary phenomenon, was not even seriously investigated by economists until the 1880s. By this time many working people were prey to its depredations. An important factor in this development was increased competition from newly industrialising countries. With demand hit, employers turned to the largest element in their costs, their wages bills, and sought to reduce them. The growing uncertainty of employment and pressure on wages led to a search for greater security. One of the first examples of this move away from reciprocity was a call from Lloyd Jones in the *Beehive*, in July 1874, urging Northumbrian miners to press for minimum wages.

New Unionism

Whilst Henry Broadhurst, Lib-Lab MP and secretary of the TUC's parliamentary committee, until his enforced retirement in 1890, held to the Gladstonian gospel of reciprocity and self-help, others shifted their position. Not all were prepared to share the view of Tom Mann, an ASE member and 'New Union' leader, and see the changing situation in terms of capitalist exploitation, the diagnosis of the recently formed Social Democratic Federation, of which he was a member. But 'New Model Unions' certainly shared his concern about unemployment and employer pressure.

Unskilled workers were particularly hard hit by unemployment in the 1880s. By 1886, however, an upturn began, encouraging workers to combine to press for improvements in wage levels, and drying up sources of strike-breaking blackleg labour. A mistitled National Labour Federation was founded on Tyneside in 1886. This was followed by another North East creation, the National Amalgamated Sailors' and Firemen's Union, in 1887. In 1888 came the London match-girls' strike and, the year after, strikes and moves to unionisation by gasworkers and dockworkers in various parts of the country.

These moves were not just bids for economic improvements, the replacement of 12 hour shifts with an eight hour day for the gasworkers and the docker's tanner for the London dockworkers, but for the respectability and status that union membership conferred. This had long been denied semi and unskilled workers by the perceived impossibility of organising them. The strikes of these years proved that this was not necessarily the case. This was partly because of technological change. New machinery required new skills from previously casual labourers. This was certainly true on the docks, where the advent of steamships meant that men needed particular expertises, thus giving them more regular employment and wage levels more likely to enable them to pay union dues. New technology also created new jobs for the previously unskilled. Work that had once been part of the turner's job, for example, now became the separate skill of the capstan spinners, who formed their own union.

Changes in technology also started to erode the distance between skilled and unskilled. In Aberdeen, in 1898, the secretary of the local branch of the Ironmoulders' Union unwittingly admitted, 'in a moulding shop it was a difficult matter to define what was really moulding work and what was labourers'.[6] The introduction of the American system of unskilled men supervised by craftsmen from the 1870s in certain industries also helped to erode this distance. In some trades this led to skilled unions countenancing the formation of separate labourers' unions as a way of maintaining demarcation lines. In others, such as the construction industry the 'New Unions', however, received little encouragement.

The impact of New Unionism

The climate, meanwhile, rapidly turned against them. Union formations continued into the 1890s. In 1891 the Co-operative movement, which had long argued against the need for its own workers to be organised, allowed the Amalgamated Society of Co-operative Employees to be set up. In 1892 the Tax Clerks' Federation was founded, whilst a dispute in Manchester in 1893 led to the establishment of the Musicians' Union. However, the 1890s also soon saw an employers' backlash against the 'New Unions'. The public support which had helped to ensure the dockers' success in 1889 was conspicuously absent a year later when the new union's power was effectively broken. The gasworkers' union survived, but not without difficulties. Its leader, Will Thorne, was a member of the SDF. He shared Burns' view of the older unions as sectional and focussed on benefits to the detriment of the struggle to improve workers' conditions by winning concessions from employers. He therefore aimed to make his union a general, not a sectional union, and determined that there should be no benefits other than strike pay.

This plan began to go awry almost straight away. Unsuccessful strike action at the end of 1889 cost the new union £10,000. Thorne was forced to institute a policy of avoiding strikes if at all possible. He also reluctantly conceded the full range of benefits, because the membership demanded it. Aspiring to the respectability of the older unions, rather than the socialist intentions of the leaders of many of the new ones was, initially at least, more important to the members. Meanwhile, progress towards a more general status was slow. Many 'New Unions' had similar experiences and remained locally and sectionally based throughout the 1890s. Others wilted in the face of lockouts by the employers after trade began to deteriorate again after 1891. Even Thorne's union lost members, only recovering towards the end of the decade. The result was that 'New Unions' remained but a small portion of total union membership. In fact the main growth in union membership of 1888–91 was in the older organisations of skilled men.

There were high hopes of the 'New Unions'. Tom Mann wrote in 1890, 'Poverty can be abolished and we consider it the work of the trade unionist to do this'.[7] There spoke the man who would play a leading part in the syndicalism of twenty years later, a movement which explicitly sought to use union power for this purpose. In the event, the main result of the discontents which fuelled new unionism was to turn energies into another sort of action. These discontents were compounded by the employers' actions during the 1890s, and the unfavourable (to unions) interpretations of the courts. Will Thorne had already begun to channel his efforts to achieve socialism into political, as well as industrial action. He was one of the labour group which, in 1898, in West Ham became the first such to control a local council, using this political base to push for the eight hour day, municipalisation of tramways and improved housing. The following year the judgement in *Lyons v. Wilkins* severely restricted the rights of pickets. After several years of resisting Keir Hardie's calls for independent labour representation the TUC now voted for action. At its behest the Farringdon Hall conference was held in London in February 1900, which led to the formation of the Labour Representation Committee, the forerunner of the Labour Party.

Notes

(1) Andrew Bullen and Alan Fowler, *The Cardroom Workers Union*, (Manchester: Amalgamated Textile Workers Union, 1986), p. 34.
(2) Speaking on the Capitalist System – Motion, 16 July 1923, *House of Commons Debates*, 5th ser., vol. 166, col. 1921.
(3) *Rhondda Leader* in 1921, quoted in Stuart MacIntyre, *Little Moscows* (Croom Helm, 1980), p. 115.
(4) Smiles was himself an engineer, and also one of the lionisers. He was the author of *Lives of the Engineers*, (1860).
(5) Quoted in David Kynaston, *King Labour* (Allen and Unwin, 1976), p. 21.
(6) Quoted in Kynaston, p. 145.
(7) Quoted in Kynaston, p. 137.

Peter Catterall is the Executive Director of the Institute of Contemporary British History and visiting lecturer in History at Queen Mary and Westfield College, London.

Joyce Howson is a postgraduate student at the University of Kent.

David Howell
Origins of the ILP

There was nothing inevitable about the emergence of independent working-class politics in Britain. To understand how and why this occurred it is important to study the foundations and role of the Independent Labour Party.

The foundation conference of the Independent Labour Party was held in Bradford on 13 and 14 January 1893. Many historians have seen this meeting and the decisions made by the 120 or so delegates as a critical step towards the emergence of the modern Labour Party. This latter body was founded as the Labour Representation Committee in 1900, and took its present title six years later. The ILP became a constituent of the new organisation, whilst retaining its distinctive identity, and provided some key figures. Keir Hardie, the Scottish miner turned journalist and politician, was already the MP for West Ham South. He chaired most of the Bradford Conference and became the most celebrated of pre-1914 Labour MPs. Another ILP Scot, Ramsey MacDonald, was the LRC's first secretary, and in January 1924, became the first ever Labour Prime Minister. Throughout the 1920s a high proportion of Labour MPs carried ILP membership cards, often a link with the political organisation that had brought them into socialist politics. For almost four decades the ILP stood at the centre of the political changes and choices that made the Labour Party into one of the major political parties. It provided personnel, ideas and a broad political style. Yet the birth of the ILP was a complex and uncertain affair and must be placed in the context of late-Victorian party politics and trade unionism.

The ILP grew from the bottom upwards. It was not the creation of a few would-be political leaders, nor did it emerge as the inevitable outcome of economic changes. It was the result of a range of initiatives taken in communities by men and women, in each case responding to the opportunities and the difficulties posed by their local environment. These developments can be traced in Scotland from 1888, in the West Riding woollen towns and in Lancashire during 1891–92.

Much of the spadework was carried out by Joseph Burgess, once a cottonworker than a journalist, through his weekly newspaper, *The Workman's Times*. In April 1892 Burgess wrote a leading article on the need for an ILP. For the rest of the year he pursued his objective with tenacity. His newspaper listed readers sympathetic to the idea and carried reports of the activities of local ILPs. When the 1892 TUC met that September in Glasgow, an informal meeting of sympathisers formed an Arrangements Committee to organise a conference. The result was the decisive Bradford meeting. Hardie recalled, more than twenty years later, the delegates' optimism:

> They were for the most part in the heyday of life, for whom 'difficulties' and 'doubts' had not been born. There was a cause to be fought for, a battle to be won ...[1]

Perhaps the memory was idealised, yet the delegates were generally young, and the attempt to build an Independent Labour Party was itself a demonstration of optimism. The decisions that they made can be understood only in the wider political and trade unions contexts.

Political spaces and industrial bases

If the champions of Independent Labour politics were to be successful they had to find space in the existing system. The character of the parliamentary franchise in the 1890s is a subject of debate. The qualifying criteria were numerous, complex and at the margins disputed in their application. Most obviously the criteria excluded all women and at any election between 1885 and December 1910, about 40% of adult males. A minority of men were plural voters on account of property or educational qualifications. What remains in doubt is how far the excluded males were largely working class. If this were the case, it is still debatable how far this handicapped the prospects for an Independent Labour initiative. Many of the excluded might well have been casually employed men who did not belong to trade unions. They were not the most obvious recruits as Labour supporters.

Britain might have been much less than a thorough electoral democracy, but it was, in the 1890s, a relatively liberal political system. There was little of the harsh repression of working-class political organisations and trade unionism that could occur in Russia, Germany, Italy and periodically in the United States. There was no memory of anything approaching the treatment of the Communards twenty years earlier in France. Such relative tolerance made liberal principles attractive and meaningful to many working-class leaders and activists. Working-class Conservatism was a powerful force especially in some locations such as Lancashire. But most trade union officials and working class politicians saw themselves in the 1880s as Radical Liberals. Those who wished to develop an independent politics had to confront the continuing strengths of this politics. There is much debate about how far the emergence of the ILP and subsequently of the Labour Party represented a clear and potentially socialist break with Liberalism – a controversy which has become one facet of a much wider debate about the inexorability or otherwise of Labour's growth to the status of a major party.

A Liberal heritage

Certainly many who played major parts in the formation and the early years of the ILP had previously been Radical Liberals. Hardie and MacDonald are well-known examples. When they became active in the ILP, they nevertheless retained many of their earlier Liberal enthusiasms, such as Free Trade, Land Reform and Irish Home Rule. Early ILP members sometimes portrayed themselves as socialists who were nevertheless the true heirs to a principled liberalism that had often been betrayed by the practices of official Liberals. From this vantage point the ILP interpretation of socialism could be characterised as a natural extension of liberal politics. Yet the fact of establishing separate political machinery inevitably meant conflict with the Liberal Party. Electoral clashes heightened hostilities which were often charged with social tensions. The establishment of separate party machinery was more than an organisational matter; it was also a statement that working-class people could work out their own solutions without middle-class intermediary.

Throughout the debates leading up to the ILP's formation and through its early years, activists evinced a deep concern that the fruits of their campaigning could be annexed by official Liberalism, or manipulated by Tory sympathisers for partisan purposes. Past conflicts had produced a deep suspicion of 'wire-pullers'; this time it would be different.

The emergence of the ILP must be located within the specific political contexts of its areas of relative strength. The delegates at the foundation conference included many from Bradford and other West Riding woollen towns. This was not a consequence of the Conference's location; rather the delegates met in Bradford on account of its position in Independent Labour politics. W. H. Drew, President of the Bradford Labour Union, had made the point in the columns of the *Workman's Times*: '… you cockneys ought to unbend, and come say to Bradford, a central town where you will find plenty of food for reflection.'[2]

Early centres of strength

Early ILP strength in the woollen belt was the consequence of economic, political and personal factors. The dominant industry was coming under pressure from overseas competition and American tariffs. The industry was weakly unionised and in the winter of 1890–91, workers at the large Manningham Mills in Bradford embarked on a long and unsuccessful strike against wage cuts. The dispute acquired a political edge as local politicians and police combined to prevent the strikers holding public meetings. One post-mortem commented: 'The operatives have from the first been fought not only by their own employers at Manningham, but by the whole of the monied class of Bradford.'[3]

One rapid consequence was the formation of the Bradford Labour Union, after the Bradford ILP. Many of its leading figures such as Fred Jowett, later a minister in the 1924 Labour government, were committed socialists who worked to develop a local organisation that was principled, independent and yet responded creatively to the immediate needs of Bradford people. They were helped by the often reactionary character of Bradford Liberalism. This was influenced heavily by local employers and the Liberal Party machine felt little need to respond positively to demands from local working-class activists. The latter could not command the resources of a major trade union and electorally Bradford Liberalism seemed relatively secure. Its grandees felt little need to make concessions either on policy or over working-class candidates. In the 1892 general election Alfred Illingworth, the epitome of the Liberal millocracy, was opposed in his West Bradford constituency by Ben Tillett, who had played a leading role in the 1889 London dock strike. Tillett's later politics were erratic but in July 1892, backed by the Bradford Labour Union, he symbolised the growing confidence of Bradford's working-class activists. Illingworth retained his seat but Tillet's poll was impressive.

Scotland and Lancashire

Bradford's claim to be the cradle of the ILP could be contested by Scotland. No individual was more evocative of the rise of the ILP than Keir Hardie and in terms of organisational developments, Scotland preceded England. By the late 1880s, Scottish Liberalism was experiencing some erosion of its traditional dominance. The importance within many Scottish communities of the split between Protestant and Catholic, between Scots and Irish immigrants and their descendants, meant that the controversy over Home Rule had a profound impact. Several Liberal politicians quit the party; so did a significant proportion of the electorate. Within the Scottish Liberal Party, there were also strongly radical sections concerned with issues such as land reform. The trade union movement in Scotland was limited and Liberal politicians saw little need to respond to the demands of organised labour. It was in this context that Hardie stood as an Independent Labour candidate at Mid-Lanark in April 1888. His vote was small but this intervention led rapidly to the formation of the Scottish Labour Party, a broad coalition of Radicals, Socialists, land reformers and trade unionists. The extent of its independence from Liberalism over the next few years was often uncertain. This organisational initiative was not matched by popular support, as in the woollen towns. The few SLP candidates in the 1892 general election polled poorly. Yet the SLP survived to send delegates to the Bradford Conference.

Another early example of Independent Labour growth could be found in Lancashire, especially in and around Manchester and in some of the cotton towns. Ethnic and religious tensions between English and the Irish helped to produce a vigorous tradition of working-class Toryism which catered for the cultural prejudices of the indigenous population. Liberalism was on the defensive and, electorally, was often unsuccessful. This perhaps gave more scope for Independent Labour initiatives, but activists had to cater for the tastes of converts from Toryism as well as from Liberalism. One symptom can be found in the politics of Robert Blatchford, the ex-soldier turned journalist who founded the Socialist weekly *The Clarion*, in Manchester late in 1891. Its style was far removed from the dour earnestness of Hardie's paper the *Labour Leader*. Instead Blatchford and his colleagues offered a culture of 'cakes and ale', with theatre and sports columns presented in a chatty style. Significantly Blatchford's best selling book, putting the case for socialism, was called *Merrie England*. Perhaps the approach showed an awareness of the need to appeal to a Lancastrian working-class that was often estranged from the puritanical side of Radical Liberalism. Moreover, the Manchester and Salford ILP, founded in the Spring of 1892, took a firm stand on the prospect of support for any other party. The celebrated Fourth Clause of the Manchester Party's Constitution simply ruled this out – a more thorough prohibition than the Bradford insistence on independence. This was not simply a matter of Mancunion fidelity to socialism. In a city where many workers were strongly Tory, there had been no suspicion that the ILP harboured Liberal sympathies.

The ILP and Trade Unions

The pioneers of Independent Labour politics had to come to terms with the prior existence of a relatively effective trade unionism amongst a minority of largely male workers. Some unions, most notably the miners, were led by men who had a firm commitment to the Liberal Party. In some constituencies miners were sufficiently numerous to dominate the electorate, and to persuade local Liberal Associations to select miners as Liberal candidates. Skilled craftswork-ers often found joint political action almost irrelevant; their strength in the workplace could seem sufficient. Once again the leaders of these unions were often Liberals. Such political attachments could make the project of an Independent Labour Party seem, at best, superfluous and often antagonistic.

Advocates of such a project needed support from the trade unions and they could find some grounds for optimism. The positions of many skilled workers were threatened as international competition led employers to seek the introduction of new technology and changed working practices. This challenge produced major disputes in the shoe industry in 1895 and in the engineering trade in 1897–98. The massed ranks of footwear workers, let alone engineers, did not become zealous partisans of Independent Labour politics, but there was growing support amongst leaders and activists. The same was true of the railway servants who had to face authoritarian managements, almost always opposed to union recognition. Socialist influence was most obvious in the new unions of the so-called unskilled workers which mushroomed at the end of the 1880s. The London dock strike of 1889 ended with a memorable victory; the new unions seemed both radical and successful. Yet their decline was as precipate as their meteoric rise. The ILP was formed as a counter-attack by employers saw new union membership plummet. Some organisations collapsed; others survived, much diminished and shorn of much of their radicalism. Yet the latter often provided leaders sympathetic to the construction of an Independent Labour politics.

Trade union politics in the 1890s was a complex and shifting business. There was a kaleidoscope of opinions indicating generational, organisational and occupational differences, as much as disputes over the desirability of political independence for labour. Those seeking the latter had to come to terms with this complexity.

Social strategies

The pioneers not only had to reckon with the complexities of trade union and community politics. They also had to face problems of socialist strategy. Some who entered the ILP, for example Fred Jowett, had been involved in the Socialist League. This group's most famous figure had been the designer and writer William Morris. From its foundation in 1884 its guiding principle had been that a socialist society was feasible, only if sufficient people were committed socialists. The first task was to make socialists by propaganda and by example, and to live as socialists. Electoral politics was a blind alley that offered no challenge to the existing order. Morris certainly believed that at some stage there would have to be a confrontation between the forces of socialism and of reaction, but for the moment, the task of the League was to stick firmly to its principles. Eventually the League disintegrated into disputatious factions but something of its moral ethos survived into the early years of the ILP:

'Nothing is too hard for their members in their virgin enthusiasm to do. They run their little prints, they sell their stocks of pamphlets, they drop their pennies into the collecting box, the buy their ILP tea and cocoa as though they were members of an idealist Communist society.'[4]

Such activities gradually became more marginal, but the principle concern of the new party was with electoral success. Concrete benefits seemed on offer; the 'making socialists' strategy seemed slow and success often seemed elusive.

When the ILP was formed, another avowed socialist party had been in the field for a decade. The Social Democratic Federation had begun as the Democratic Federation in 1881, but had changed its name in 1884 and adopted an explicitly socialist commitment. Historians have often presented the SDF critically. It has been portrayed as sectarian, Marxist, un-British and unsuccessful. Its principal figure, the Cambridge-educated H. M. Hyndman, was often autocratic; this had been one factor producing a split and the formation by critics of the Socialist League. Yet the dominant image is misleading. The SDF presented itself as the British equivalent of the explicit socialist parties that were emerging elsewhere in Europe. This did not mean that its politics were rigid. Local branches were often pragmatic, immediate reforms were taken very seriously, and members were often active in trade unions. Especially in Lancashire where the SDF was relatively strong, socialists seem to have moved easily between the Federation and the emerging ILP. Indeed six Lancashire SDF branches sent delegates to the Bradford Conference. Yet if there was often comradeship between activists, those who came to lead the ILP were more hostile. They fostered the notion of the SDF as narrow and unsuccessful and contrasted this failure with what they took to be the broad-based appeal of the ILP. The truth was less clear cut.

Choices

These complexities provided the backcloth for the critical decisions at the Bradford Conference. Delegates rejected the option of naming the organisation the 'Socialist Labour Party' and instead favoured the option of 'Independent Labour Party'. The rationale for the choice was electoral. The party must appeal to voters who had little understanding of socialism. As a balance delegates gave the party a socialist objective – the collective ownership of the means of production, distribution and exchange. Here was a classic compromise – a Labour title and a socialist goal. The Bradford proceedings demonstrated a firm commitment to the protection of local democracy. The party had grown from the localities; it should not be taken over by the ambitious nor by anyone who would deliver the party to one of the established party machines. Yet delegates rejected the robust independence of the

Manchester Fourth Clause. The question of support for specific candidates from other parties should be left to local initiative. Delegates
adopted a brief programme, primarily of economic and social reforms,
which could be presented as early steps towards the socialist objective.

The democratic sentiments of the delegates were further revealed in
the lack of any gender discrimination in membership provisions. The
ILP was open to women on the same terms as men and in the early
years prominent women socialists – Katherine St John Conway, Carrie
Martyn and Enid Stacey – were active as party propagandists. Yet
formal rules and party practice often differed. Women, particularly
from the working class, faced formidable economic and social obstacles to regular participation in party work. Moreover when these barriers were surmounted, they could find themselves limited to
traditional women's activities within the organisation. The underlying tensions would be revealed in the early 1900s as the movement
for women's suffrage expanded and ILP members had to decide on its
importance relative to their other concerns.

This example indicates that, in 1893, delegates only provided the
skeleton for a new party. Much would depend on how formal decisions were translated into political practice. Indeed in the first year the
party as a national body barely functioned. The initial structure
proved unwieldy. Financial provisions were inadequate. The second
conference at Manchester, in February 1894, took key decisions on
organisational reform and personnel ensuring a more durable and
effective party. As the 1892–95 Liberal government increasingly
appeared to drift, so the ILP vote at some by-elections seemed promis-
ing. But hopes of a swift breakthrough proved illusory. At the 1895
general election the ILP ran 28 candidates. This test proved beyond the
party's organisational resources. All were defeated, often with poor
votes. With the loss of Hardie's seat, the ILP had no parliamentary
presence.

From ILP to Labour

After 1895 membership declined and by-election performances were
often disappointing. In 1898 and 1899 the ILP fought no parliamentary
contests; only limited successes in local government provided evidence of achievement. Much of the early and vigorous local democracy was ebbing. The ILP had developed a leadership group,
sometimes known as the 'Big Four'. Alongside Hardie and
MacDonald, there was the Yorkshireman Philip Snowden, later
Chancellor of the Exchequer in the first two Labour governments. By
the late 1890s he had developed the ethical propaganda of the ILP into
a fine rhetorical art. The quartet was completed by another Scot, Bruce
Glasier, once active in the Socialist League and by the late 1890s, the

quintessential ILP propagandist. This group had a thorough distaste for any close connection with the SDF and in 1897–98 succeeded, not without some manipulation, in blocking moves for the fusion of the two bodies into a United Socialist party. Gasier's justification for this utilised a stereotype that became later a misleading commonplace amongst historians:

> ...the ways of the SDF are not our ways ... the ways of the SDF are more doctrinaire, more Calvinistic, more aggressively sectarian than the ILP. The SDF have failed to touch the heart of the people.[5]

This caricature ignored how in some Lancashire towns ILP and SDF members worked harmoniously together. But the defeat of the United Socialist option left the way open for the ILP membership's preferred strategy – an alliance with the trade unions. Initially the ILP had flirted with the possibility of organising to remove old-style Liberal trade union leaders, and to replace them with political sympathisers. Success had been limited and, by the late 1890s, ILP leaders effectively accepted that they must deal with existing union leaderships. This pragmatism helped to produce the Labour Representation Committee in 1900.

The circumstances of the ILP's birth and of its early years show the problems facing advocates of socialist and independent working-class politics in Britain. How should ILP members relate to and work with trade unions? How could they find space within a party system with well-established mass parties? What were the prospects for socialists in the world's first industrial capitalist society with all the legacies of economic and political power that this entailed. The agendas was forbidding; the answers developed by early ILP members were controversial. Yet the emphasis on the difficulties of their task only serves to highlight their achievement. The formation and the survival of the political creativity of a group of men and women, mostly young and mostly working-class. There was nothing natural or inevitable about this party; it had to be built.

Notes

(1) *Labour Leader*, 9 April 1914.
(2) *Workingman's Times*, 13 August 1892.
(3) *Yorkshire Factory Times*, 1 May 1891.
(4) *Seedtime*, July 1894.
(5) *Independent Labour Party Conference Report*, 1898, p. 27.

David Howell is Professor of Government at the University of Manchester

Duncan Tanner
New Liberalism and Social Reform

Duncan Tanner argues that the Liberals' reforms (1906–14) were not an indication that the party was on the verge of collapse, vainly trying to consolidate a threatened position.

Since George Dangerfield's classic tirade, *The Strange Death of Liberal England* (1935) political historians have commonly seen the Liberals' reforms of 1906–14 as a pragmatic and doomed attempt at propping up their increasingly threatened position on the left of British politics. Reforms came after pressure from the Labour Party or the Civil Service. A party whose reforming instincts were all imported rested on weak foundations. The Liberal Party was thus easily swept away.

Other historians (particularly after the publication of Peter Clarke's seminal work, *Lancashire and the New Liberalism* in 1971) found this image difficult to reconcile with the facts. Between 1906 and 1914, they argued, the Liberal Party put forward a programme of reforms without precedent in the nineteenth century and without equal until 1945. The programme had three facets: State provision of a welfare safety net (particularly through old age pensions and health and unemployment insurance); minimum wage rates in certain industries to improve earnings; and taxation of the rich to finance the welfare reforms. The inspiration for the shift in policy was a shift in ideology. *Laissez-faire* Liberalism gave way to the 'new Liberalism', which saw greater merit in State intervention. Government ministers who sympathised with aspects of this approach, or who found it politically useful, supplied the will to pass legislation. In the light of this interpretation, can we still see the Liberals' reforms as a pragmatic device to revive their declining fortunes? Should we still see the Liberal Party as an organisation on the brink of collapse? Or should we give the party a clean bill of health?

The origins of reform

In the 1880s and 1890s, Liberals (and others) began to discuss the need for greater State intervention and more social reform. The most radical prospectus was that of the 'New Liberals', the most important of whom were the economist J.A. Hobson and the sociologist L.T. Hobhouse. Both were also journalists and active propagandists in favour of reconstructing Liberal politics. They argued that in the past the Liberal Party had been too concerned with individual liberty. The economic conditions which caused a morally reprehensible degree of inequality and disadvantage had consequently not been tackled. Moreover, social conditions effectively removed the real liberty of the poorer sections of society to have an adequate standard of living and hence to lead a decent life. The New Liberals' answer was State intervention of two kinds. First, State-enacted social reforms, designed to assist those without employment. Second, State-imposed minimum wages to ensure that those with jobs were paid an adequate amount.

The New Liberals mixed and discussed with Labour and Socialist intellectuals, and sought their political and electoral co-operation. Yet they saw themselves as Liberal collectivists, and attacked many Marxist arguments. Reforms which aimed to promote real liberty and social harmony, they argued, were morally just and fundamentally Liberal. Theirs was a sophisticated Liberal case for State intervention.

Other Liberals supported reform for rather different reasons. Social surveys by men such as Booth and Rowntree demonstrated that most poverty was not caused by deficiencies in an individual's character, as some Liberals had once argued, but by old age, low wages and large families. In taking this line, they were reflecting what many Liberal activists on the ground knew already: that environmental conditions beyond an individual's control influence the ability of men, and especially of women, children and the elderly, to control their lives. The New Liberals thus drew support from often religiously inspired party members, who regarded the absence of attempts to tackle poverty as a moral wrong. In some parts of the country, religious radicals of this kind dominated Liberal politics. In London, they developed a highly interventionist municipal programme during the 1890s which became a model for reformers across the country.

Most Liberals had not shifted this far to the left. Nonetheless, the idea that certain functions were best provided by the community had been gaining ground in both parties since the 1870s. The provision of parks, schools, transport, water and gas supply, sanitation, poor relief and other social facilities by the municipality had increased local expenditure by around 300% by the turn of the century.[1] Contemporaries wrote of 'municipal socialism', and the tendency of local authorities 'to provide everything the population required in its passage from the cradle to the grave.' Even very traditional Liberal local authorities had often acknowledged the need for greater intervention of some kind by 1900.

Support for reform amongst moderate reformers was not confined to questions of municipal intervention. Many increasingly recognised that the State should take some responsibility for tackling some social evils. There was growing support for the introduction of old age pensions. Some, concerned that a physically poor workforce was inefficient at a time when foreign economic competition was making British goods seem less competitive, were willing to go further.

These moderate reformers developed, in some instances, a careful justification of their opinions. They were notably more cautious than the New Liberals and their allies about the scale and extent of State intervention. They were particularly concerned about the New Liberals' pro-labour inclinations, and about reforms which might increase industries' wage costs. Although a change in economic theory suggested to some that wages could be increased without harming the economy, moderate Liberals were almost instinctively sceptical about reforms which could determine the profitability of manufacturing industry and hence the prosperity of the nation.[2]

Financing reform

The means by which Liberals hoped to finance reform are very important in assessing the nature and direction of policy. Unlike the Tories, they could not contemplate taxes on imported goods ('tariff reform'). Free Trade was the Liberals' sacred cow, the policy which had brought economic prosperity and electoral success. At the same time, however, many Liberals — even many Liberal reformers — did not wish to increase income tax considerably in order to pay the costs of State welfare. To do so would only undermine the nation's prosperity by reducing the wealth of the most productive elements in society. Moderate reformers were thus torn between a belief in reform and a faith in economic views which suggested that 'productive' wealth should not labour under too many constraints.

The Liberal Party made some progress towards tackling this problem in the 1890s. By extending an economic analysis developed earlier in the century, they drew a distinction between 'productive' and 'unproductive' wealth, and decided to raise money by taxing the latter. Thus in 1894–95 Sir William Harcourt, Liberal Chancellor in the brief Liberal ministry of 1892–95, introduced death duties on larger incomes, while actually cutting income tax for 'poorer' income tax payers. (This effectively meant aiding a portion of the middle classes. Many members of the lower middle class, and the vast majority of the working classes, did not pay income tax).

Some Liberals also revived the idea of taxing land in order to raise revenue and pay for social reforms. Taxing land, they argued, would attack the 'idle class' of aristocratic landowners. These men leased their land to others (small farmers, mineowners, industrialists, shopkeepers) and lived off the spoils of their largely inherited property. As a 'parasitic' class, landowners, and their wealth, were a legitimate target for Liberals. Support for land reform became so extensive in this period that more than 200 Liberal MPs joined a parliamentary group to promote land legislation following the 1906 election.[3]

New Liberals, while sharing many of these views, were willing to push reform further and to increase income taxes more dramatically to pay for State expenditure. The New Liberal economist, J.A. Hobson, argued that by diverting money to those who would purchase goods — the working class — the economy would be assisted not hindered. There was, he argued, no economic reason to fear such a policy. Neither was it ideologically questionable. Taxation of the rich, and the consequent welfare expenditure, was not Socialist, but Liberal. As the New Liberal theorist and future Cabinet Minister, Herbert Samuel, put it 'all expenditure which succeeds in improving the part benefits not that part alone, but the whole of the community. This is why all sections may justly be called upon to share the cost of measures which in their direct and immediate application touch only the well-being of the poorer.'[4] This was not Socialist *class* legislation, but Liberal reforms, designed to help one section of an interconnected 'organic' community.

Liberal theorists and politicians were developing their case for intervention long before the formation of the Labour Party in 1900. There were disagreements over the extent of reform, and over how far reforms should affect the affairs, and the money, of industrialists. There were, of course, a large number of Liberals who were wary about reform, and some who were willing to swallow their doubts because of the party's evident need to capture more working class votes — the party had, after all, been in the electoral wilderness for much of the period since 1886. The Liberal Party was moving towards a reforming programme, but it had not been dramatically converted to the New Liberals' radical vision.

Liberal reforms 1906-14

The reforms which the Liberals introduced, or attempted to introduce after 1906, were a compromise between the varying views of the reforming elements of the 1890s, although the detailed aspects of the programme were not thrashed out in advance. Very little legislation stemmed directly from labour pressure. Most of the exceptions concerned trade union political and industrial rights and similar issues, rather than social reforms. The most notable of these exceptions were the Trade Disputes Act of 1906, the Trade Union Act of 1913 (which allowed unions the right to establish political funds following a ballot of members) and the legislation which introduced State payment of MPs. Liberals listened to Labour views in favour of, and sometimes *against*, State intervention, and incorporated some of their demands into their social and labour legislation. Although New Liberals used

Labour expansion and industrial unrest after 1906 to persuade more moderate colleagues of the need for further reform, the actual legislation reflected Liberal views and beliefs on most occasions.

The reforming impetus accelerated dramatically after 1908, when Asquith became Prime Minister, Lloyd George became Chancellor of the Exchequer, and Winston Churchill became President of the Board of Trade. Under their guidance, the Liberal Party consolidated and extended its shift towards reform. The most important reforms were the old age pensions legislation (1908) and the National Insurance Act (1911). In passing two major welfare reforms in such close proximity, the Liberals broke dramatically away from past precedent. Yet the legislation itself was hardly revolutionary. The State pension was free, but not universal. It was limited to people aged over 70 whose incomes were less than £31.10s. (£31.50) per year. It was also subject to a character test. Only around half a million of the oldest, poorest, and most sober elderly people obtained a pension, which, at 5s (25p) per week was a pound less than a bare subsistence income. Sickness and unemployment benefits of 10s. (50p) per week were also insufficient for full maintenance, and only available to those in particular industries who kept up their weekly contributions.[5] New Liberals had wanted insurance benefits to be free and universal, and pensions to be more generous, but moderate reformers and party traditionalists blocked these proposals. On social reform, the Liberals had a good record compared to previous governments, but they were still open to criticism.

The second important facet of the Liberal reforms concerned the party's minimum wage legislation. The 1909 Trade Boards Act built on ideas and discoveries from before 1906.[6] The legislation covered around half a million workers in sweated trades such as box and chain-making, tailoring and lace-making. The government introduced a miners' minimum wage in 1912, and was about to introduce a minimum wage for agricultural labourers when war broke out in 1914.

The details of the minimum wage legislation reflected the Liberal concern that industry should not bear too heavy a burden. Minimum wage rates were to vary between areas, in accordance with local conditions and profitability, and were set at a low level. New Liberals were not content with this, arguing in 1912, that 'the time has come to have in mind as a distinct object of Liberal policy the general principle of a living wage for every worker.'[7] They were not opposed to nationalising certain industries if employers could not run them in the interests of workers and the community, but there was considerable opposition in the Liberal Party to both these aspects of their ideas when legislation was being discussed. Here again compromises between New Liberals and moderate reformers ensured that, as on social reform, Liberals were open to criticism from the left.

The third facet of the Liberal reforms concerned the finance of State intervention. Lloyd George's 'People's Budget' of 1909 extended the taxation of the rich begun by Harcourt in the 1890s. He introduced land taxes and increased income tax, super tax and death duties. However, and in part because of opposition from within his party, Lloyd George was unable to take these ideas as far as he wished. The Budget was so constructed that the lower middle class escaped increased taxation, while taxes on spirits and tobacco hit the working class much harder.[8]

The balance sheet

In moving even this far to the left, Liberal reformers had met serious opposition. For some the party had gone too far. In 1910 around 25 MPs stood down rather than support the Liberal programme.[9] In the main, however, the Liberals managed to move some way to the left on social and economic matters without losing all their rural and middle-class support. They also maintained their support for political aims much beloved of orthodox Liberals, such as Welsh Disestablishment, Home Rule and Constitutional reform. Indeed, on some occasions (as with the battle for the People's Budget in 1909) 'radical' and 'traditional' interests were merged together. The traditional Liberals' oppoosition to the undemocratic aristocracy became inflamed when the Lords rejected the budget. The campaign in favour of the budget was thus also a campaign against the Lords. Economic and constitutional reform, the 'New' and the 'Old' Liberalism, came together. By 1914 the Liberals had created a working-class electoral base of its own and secured the co-operation of Labour. They were, in addition, able to win electoral victories in some fairly middle-class constituencies, and to hold a number of rural areas. This was an achievement unmatched by Labour except in 1945.

The Liberal Party was nonetheless not without weaknesses. It was difficult to keep such a coalition together, so as to satisfy all its supporters. The Liberals' social reforms were frequently toned down. Their labour and economic reforms were restrained by concerns about taxing industrial wealth. 'Unproductive' wealth was a legitimate target, but beyond this Liberals had to proceed cautiously. If the economic situation had been worse, some Liberals would no doubt have been much less enthusiastic about State intervention. In the longer term this made the Liberals vulnerable to attack from the left (which is not to say that the *extent* of their decline was inevitable). Yet despite these potential weaknesses, the Liberals were a powerful force in 1914. Labour often supported both 'radical' and 'traditional' Liberal policies. It had exposed small weaknesses in the Liberals' appeal, but had few alternatives which seemed credible to the electorate. It was not on the verge of replacing the Liberal Party. On the contrary, it remained a junior ally (albeit one with greater ambitions).[10]

A study of the Liberal reforms of 1906–14 does not suggest that the party was on the verge of collapse, but neither does it suggest that the New Liberalism had effected its complete recovery. Through this qualified verdict on the Edwardian Liberal reforms, we are in a better position to understand the nature of the Liberals' achievement, the causes of their post-war decline, and some of the problems which they have subsequently faced in trying to recover their position as the major anti-Tory force in British politics.

Notes

(1) Offer, A. *Property and Politics 1870–1914* (Cambridge University Press, 1981), Chapter 15.

(2) As in Six Oxford Men *Essays in Liberalism* (Cassell & Co, 1897).

(3) Murray, B.K. *The People's Budget 1909–10* (Clarendon, 1980) p.46.

(4) ibid., p.35.

(5) Vinson, A. 'The Edwardians and poverty' in Read, D (ed.), *Edwardian England* (Historical Association/Croom Helm, 1982) pp.84—5.

(6) The most influential social investigators were the Rowntrees. See Rowntree, B.S. Poverty. *A Study of Town Life* (Macmillan, 1901) and Rowntree, B.S. and Kendall, M. *How the Labourer Lives. A Study of Rural Poverty* (Thomas Nelson, 1913).

(7) Memo by H.W. Massingham, J. Rowntree, J.A. Hobson, L.T. Hobhouse, P. Alden, B.S. Rowntree, E.R. Cross, A.S. Rowntree to the Cabinet, 20 May 1912 (Lloyd George Ms LG C/21/1/17).

(8) Murray, *People's Budget*, pp. 170, 292–5.

(9) Blewett, N. *The Peers, the Parties and the People. The General Elections of 1910* (Macmillan, 1972) p.215.

(10) The electoral and institutional strengths and weaknesses of the Liberal Party also have to be taken into account in assessing the causes of decline. For a complete interpretation and analysis, Tanner, D.M. *Political Change and the Labour Party 1900–18* (Cambridge University Press, 1990).

Duncan Tanner lectures in History at University College of North Wales, Bangor.

Martin Pugh

Votes for Women

Did the enfranchisement of women in Britain result from the militant activities of the suffragettes before the First World War? Martin Pugh reconsiders the factors that led to the inclusion of women in the 1918 Representation of the People Act.

Who or what contributed most to the eventual granting of the franchise to women? The answer that springs most readily to mind concerns the campaigns of Emmeline Pankhurst and her daughters, Christable and Sylvia, between 1905 and 1914. This is hardly surprising: all movements like to have heroes and martyrs. The images of suffragettes being manhandled by police, undergoing hunger strikes and forcible feeding in prison, and in the case of Emily Wilding Davison, meeting a violent death for the cause, are too indelible to be easily forgotten. Moreover, the Pankhursts possessed a talent for self-publicity which they exercised for years after the campaign had ended.[1]

But history is an unsentimental business, and careful analysis of the activities of the militant suffragettes has gone a long way to exploding the extravagant claims made by their leaders about their role in winning the vote. In particular three qualifications about their significance can be made. First, not only did militant methods fail to shake the government's view on women's suffrage, they actually alienated, if only temporarily, some of the support for the cause as is clear from the shifting pattern of voting in Parliament (see Table 1).

1911 Conciliation Bill:	Conservative	Liberal	Labour	Irish	Total
For	53	145	26	31	255
Against	43	36	0	9	88
1912 Conciliation Bill:					
For	63	117	25	33	208
Against	114	73	0	35	222
1917 Representation of the People Bill:					
For	140	184	30	33	387
Against	45	12	0	0	57

Table 1. MP's Votes on Women's Suffrage Bill

Second, Pankhurst claims to have won over public opinion scarcely seem consistent with the growing hostility shown by the crowds at their meetings, the defeat of their candidate at the Bow and Bromley by-election in 1912, and the deep gulf between them and working-class women. Always a small organisation, the Women's Social and Political Union repeatedly split until it became a mere rump of those who were willing to give unquestioning loyalty to the Pankhursts.[2] Third, during the critical period 1916–18 when enfranchisement was actually being achieved, the Pankhursts had abandoned their campaign for women and exercised little influence except, perhaps, as a memory; none of them returned to womens' causes again.

If research has undermined the significance of militancy it has also demonstrated that the women's movement had a longer history and a wider range of concerns than concentration on Edwardian suffrage campaigns would suggest. Since 1866 the non-militant suffragists had campaigned in conjunction with allies like the Liberal MP John Stuart Mill, who seized the opportunity offered by the debates on the Second Reform Bill to make women's suffrage a serious question. No doubt these suffragists were largely middle-class, and they never won more than a few thousand members until about 1909. Therefore they remained vulnerable to the accusation that they did not represent the views of ordinary women who, it was claimed, were largely indifferent to the need for a vote. However, it has become clear that the decades during which they laboured quietly by means of meetings, pamphlets, petitions and bills regularly introduced by friendly backbenchers were, in fact, years of considerable progress for the cause. So much so that by the beginning of the new century a majority of MPs had become supporters, if rather lukewarm ones, of women's suffrage.

Separate spheres

Yet one should not assume that such shifts of opinion were the result simply of the efforts of the organised movement. Millicent Fawcett, the leading suffragist, always argued that when the vote was attained it would be as a consequence of wider changes in society affecting women. There is clearly something in this. Most Victorians saw the claim for the vote in the context of their broader social and political attitudes. Conventionally the sexes were considered to inhabit two distinct spheres — one the world of work, politics and war occupied by men, the other the world of home, children and morality for which women were destined by nature and by God.[3] Many people have never entirely surrendered such ideas. However, the achievement of the late Victorian period was to demonstrate that women might in fact participate in the male sphere without necessarily subverting the existing social system. For example, women made great advances at all levels of education in this period and, thereby, won a wider share of employment especially in the fast expanding white collar sector where they often performed the same work as men.

From the 1880s thousands of women also joined organisations attached to the political parties. There they became essential as the volunteer activists organising social events, canvassing voters, making platform speeches and often playing leadership roles. In the long run this proof of competence in the male sphere, and of loyalty to party, materially reduced the fears of politicians about enfranchising women.[4] Many Victorian women advanced towards a public role by a route that began with voluntary work for churches, charities and poor law visiting, and led at length to a new and formal position in local government after 1869. Not only did women ratepayers become voters, they were even elected to school boards, poor law boards, parish councils and, after 1907, county councils.[5]

In the short term such advances could be seen as absorbing women's energies and thereby diverting them from seeking the parliamentary vote. But in the long run their participation in local government made women's exclusion from national elections increasingly untenable. Developments of this sort are easily overlooked because they produced no sudden or obvious leap towards the parliamentary vote. Their effect can only really be appreciated in terms of generational changes. Mid-Victorians, to whom Mill's proposals in 1867 had appeared very radical, were simply replaced by the Edwardian generation which took for granted a somewhat wider role for women, and which had less reason to fear that women's political interests would detract from their conventional role as wives and mothers.

Political dilemmas

There is, thus, a case for saying that by the early 1900s the debate over the general principle of enfranchising women had been largely won. This, however, by no means resolved the problem, for several further political obstacles had to be overcome. First, politiciians had yet to be convinced that women's suffrage mattered enough to the majority of women to justify devoting scarce parliamentary time to it. Up to a point Mrs Fawcett's non-militants helped to persuade them by mobilising more trade unions behind the cause, and by their shrewd electoral pact with the Labour Party in 1912; this put real pressure on the Asquith government both by threatening more Labour candidates in Liberal constituencies, and by encouraging a drift of Liberal women towards Labour.[6] In addition, Fawcett's National Union of Women's Suffrage Societies at last began to grow into something like a mass organisation. From under 6,000 in 1907 membership rose to over

50,000 by 1913. Many of the new members were women who had been aroused by suffragette activities; while they did not wish to be involved with militant methods themselves, they felt moved to show their support for the cause in a different way. This was probably the one positive contribution of the Pankhursts to winning the vote.

A further intractable politicial problem remained. If they were to pass legislation politicians must advance from the principle of women's suffrage to the details: how many women should be enfranchised and on what qualifications? This was complicated because not all men yet enjoyed the vote, and there were still 11 ways of qualifying. Many Liberal and Labour MPs disliked the bills designed to enfranchise single women ratepayers because they thought this would present an advantage to the Conservatives by giving yet more representation to propertied people. The question of party advantage had been a central dilemma in the reforms of 1832, 1867 and 1884, and it was naïve to expect the enfranchisement of women to be any different.

The impact of war

One popular explanation for the women's eventual triumph is that the deadlock was somehow resolved by the First World War. In particular, it has been claimed that women's valuable work for the war effort radically changed male ideas about their role in society.[7] This, however, seems simplistic and even erroneous. It obviously overlooks the pre-1914 changes of attitude. It is also inconsistent with the deliberate wartime policy of ejecting women from their wartime employment and, indeed, the severe backlash against their work; during the 1920s the idea that a woman's place was in the home was as strong as it had ever been. Finally, one must take account of the process by which enfranchisement actually occurred during 1914–18. Not surprisingly votes for women simply vanished from the agenda for some time. The issue returned only because the politicians grew anxious to enfranchise more men, many of whom had lost their qualification as a result of moving home for war service. It was this that led to the scheme of parliamentary reform in 1917 in which women were included.[8]

Yet if the war had no fundamental effect, it did have a beneficial short-term impact in substituting a sympathetic Prime Minister, Lloyd George, for an anti-suffragist, Asquith, and also in creating a coalition government which wanted to find a comprehensive compromise on reform questions. Within the compromise each party got at least something that it wanted. Labour and the Liberals felt reassured by the generous grant of the vote to over eight million women — too large a number to give an advantage to the Conservatives. Equally significantly, the politicians safeguarded themselves by imposing careful terms upon the women voters; they now included married as well as single women, and limited the vote to those aged 30 years or more. In these terms one has a good indication of motive. They believed that the interests of the mature family woman would be largely confined to the domestic sphere, and would be unlikely to include radical, feminist demands. Her inclusion would thus help to promote the stability of the political system rather than the reverse.

Only when politicians felt satisfied that it was safe to do so would they extend the vote to the entire female sex who, after all, represented a majority of the population. Ultimately, then, women's enfranchisement in 1918 rested upon two underlying considerations: first it avoided presenting an obvious advantage to one party, and second it was judged likely to strengthen the British political system by widening it rather on the pattern of reform in 1832 and 1867.

Notes

(1) Pankhurst, E. Sylvia *The Suffragette Movement* (Longman, 1931); Christabel Pankhurst *Unshackled* (Hutchinson, 1959); Emmeline Pankhurst *My Own Story* (Eveleigh Nash, 1914).
(2) Liddington, J. and Norris J. *One Hand Tied Behind Us: The Rise of the Women's Suffrage Movement* (Virago, 1979) p.193, 205, 219; Rosen, A. *Rise Up Women! the militant campaign of the Women's Social and Political Union 1903–14* (Routledge and Kegan Paul, 1974).
(3) Harrison, B. *Separate Spheres: the Opposition to Women's Suffrage in Britain* (Croom Helm, 1978).
(4) Pugh, M. *Women's Suffrage in Britain 1867–1928* (Historical Association, 1980) pp.12–13.
(5) Hollis, P. *Laides Elect: Women in English Local Government 1865–1914* (Clarendon, 1987).
(6) See Hume, L.P. *The National Union of Women's Suffrage Societies 1897–1914* (Garland, 1982); S.S. Holton *Feminism and Democracy* (Cambridge University Press, 1986); M. Pugh 'Labour and women's suffrage', in Brown K., *The First Labour Party* (Croom Helm, 1985).
(7) Marwick, A. *Women at War 1914–18* (Routledge and Kegan Paul, 1977).
(8) Pugh, M. *Electoral Reform in War and Peace 1906–1918* (Routledge and Kegan Paul, 1978).

Martin Pugh is Professor of Modern British History at the University of Newcastle upon Tyne.

Sam Merry
British Foreign Policy
1894–1914

The Union of Democratic Control, set up by Liberal and Labour dissidents after the outbreak of war in 1914, was highly critical of the secret diplomatic entanglements that it felt had embroiled Britain in a general war. Sam Merry reassesses the diplomacy of the preceding years and defends the motives of Sir Edward Grey and his predecessors at the Foreign Office.

Considerations of British foreign policy under the Liberals must take account of two factors: what Lloyd George in his memoirs describes as 'a ridiculously small percentage of time devoted to foreign affairs' in Cabinet, and the secrecy with which foreign affairs were conducted up to 1912. One effect of this was the dominance of the Foreign Secretary (and Prime Minister) in Foreign Affairs and the great weight of responsibility which Sir Edward Grey (Foreign Secretary) in particular carried. Another effect was what critics of secrecy saw as irresponsibility and unaccountability, which they particularly identified in the nature of British ties with France as a result of the *Entente*.

The small amount of time devoted to foreign affairs has been attributed to consensus and continuity in the running of Foreign Affairs: the conventional view of Britain's position is that from 1894–1902 there was a gradual realisation that 'Splendid Isolation' could not be maintained with any sense of confidence, the Boer War had not been an easy war to win and from 1899 Germany was beginning to pose a potential naval threat to the Empire. Hence, from 1902, Britain began to emerge from isolation (having tried unsuccessfully to make overtures to Germany in 1899) with the Anglo-Japanese Alliance of 1902, the *Entente Cordiale* of 1904 (inherited by Grey in December 1905), the military and naval conversations with France in 1906, and the Anglo-Russian *entente* in 1907. The Triple Entente settled Britain's colonial differences with France and Russia; but at the same time Grey was at pains to emphasise the other strand of foreign policy, which was to attempt friendship with Germany by keeping her informed of developments and by trying to maintain open relations with her.

A second reason for the devotion of little time to foreign affairs was that the Committee of Imperial Defence which included some, though not all, members of the Cabinet, dealt with much business touching on

Foreign Policy. But the secrecy (normal in the running of foreign affairs) which surrounded Grey's conduct opened up Grey (and Asquith) to criticism from the isolation wing of the party who felt that they had not been treated with candour and, in the wake of the outbreak of the First World War, more widely from those who felt that the issues should have been debated in Cabinet to produce a complete overhaul of British foreign policy after the Bosnian Crisis of 1908. This, it was argued, might have averted the tragedy of war.

To the criticism of secrecy is added that of Grey's ineffectiveness. Lloyd George criticised him as the wrong man for the job: 'what was wanted was a man with high courage bordering on audacity which is the hallmark of a great minister'. Around the issue of Grey's competence is the question of whether he broke decisively with the past or whether he continued it; the answers to which lie in British policy since 1894 under Salisbury and Balfour.

'Splendid isolation'

The phrase 'splendid isolation' gained currency around 1894–95 after the conclusion of the Franco-Russian Alliance. It is particularly associated with Lord Salisbury's premiership. What was the nature — if any — of Britain's isolation? If it was 'splendid' in what sense was this true? If splendid isolation existed was it a deliberate policy, and when did it end? Several myths persist over these questions. It is true that during the winter of 1895–96 — after a succession of blows to its prestige — Britain's alleged isolation became a catchword, after Britain and Germany were involved in a press slanging match as to who was the more isolated. Indeed there was, according to C.H.D. Howard, 'probably more talk of Britain's 'isolation' in 1895 and 1896 than at any other time in the nineteenth century or the early twentieth.'

But the phrase 'splendid isolation' was first used in the Canadian Parliament by G.E. Foster (leader of the House): 'The Great Mother Empire stands splendidly isolated in Europe'. It was taken up and used by Joseph Chamberlain at a banquet in 1896 and reported in the British press at the time of the Jameson Raid. But Britain was more concerned about the dangers of isolation and the epithet 'splendid' was taken as an indication of complacency due to superiority through empire: Britain could always rely on the support of her self-governing colonies. The conclusion of the Franco-Russian Alliance and events in South Africa were simultaneously showing that 'splendid' had rather an uncertain, and therefore ironic, ring to it.

Isolation has two causes — unfriendliness on the part of neighbours, and a deliberate avoidance of 'entangling alliances' (a phrase first used in Thomas Jefferson's Inaugural Address of 1801). The latter was pursued as deliberate policy by the Americans in the nineteenth century. Although this second meaning was one that was taken up by Salisbury, the first was the usually construed meaning during this period when the phrase was first coined.

How far was isolation a deliberate policy? During Salisbury's second and third administrations Britain, often collaborated with one or more of the great European powers — with Italy over the Mediterranean agreements and with Portugal over the South African War. She drew closer to the Triple Alliance, and to Germany in particular with intervention in Africa. In fact, Salisbury tried to uphold the principle of the Concert of Europe. Did he avoid in peacetime any formal alliance entailing *casus belli*? No British government had committed Britain to war on the continent since 1870 over Belgium. But in 1899 Salisbury did give a pledge to Portugal to defend and protect all her conquests or colonies to cut off the Boer supply lines through Portuguese-controlled Lourenço Marques on Dellagoa Bay.

This agreement was not laid before Parliament; neither were the Mediterranean agreements of 1887, Salisbury's undertakings to Italy and Austria-Hungary, nor the Anglo-German conventions of 30 August 1898. Thus the idea that Britain was splendidly isolated resulted from ignorance about treaties and conventions, due to the secrecy of its conduct of foreign affairs.

Salisbury's policy

A further myth is that Salisbury originated the policy of splendid isolation (just as Chamberlain tried to end it). However, studies of Salisbury in the two decades after his death do not attribute to him any fondness for isolation. (William Harbutt Dawson first attributed it to him in 1923). Salisbury was afraid of 'dangerous isolation' and when he used the phrase he often used it ironically. He felt a keen sense of duty to 'the community of nations' and might have made a good European: 'we are part of the community of Europe, and we must do our duty as such'.

Nevertheless Salisbury did, on a number of occasions, state the classic British foreign policy stance of avoiding pledges obliging the resort to force in an unforeseen contingency. Compare his favourite constitutional justification with that given by Grey to the French in 1906:

Britain's popular and parliamentary institutions made it possible for the British government to give any assurance, engagement, pledge or promise to go to war in the future and in a hypothetical contingency, since the ultimate decision on questions of peace or war must lie with Parliament and it is impossible to see what Parliament's attitude would be should the contingency provided against happen to arise, since that would depend on the circumstances of the case and on the state of public opinion at the time.

He also used a similar line in a famous memorandum (29 May 1901) over a projected defensive alliance with Germany, refusing to tie the hands of a future parliament in questions of peace and war. This raises the question of how far Grey's policy differed from Salisbury's since the latter's administrations were not truly isolated. Salisbury sought an alliance with Germany and maintained or made alliances with Portugal and Japan. Grey's policy can be considered as a continuation of this policy with the renewal of the *Entente Cordiale* and the making of a new agreement with Russia. At the same time both Salisbury and Grey tried to avoid entangling alliances, Grey also using the 'constitutional' defence until within a few days of war. Both Grey and Salisbury tried to invoke the Concert of Europe — Grey successfully after the Balkan Wars, but unsuccessfully during the Sarajevo crisis. Both men gave a public impression of isolation by keeping essential commitments secret.

Whether Britain ever had a policy of isolation must therefore be open to question, but in so far as it did, it should not be seen as coming to an end with the Anglo-Japanese Alliance of 1902. The joint declaration with France in April 1904 under Lansdowne which gave secret undertakings to France in Morocco, should the legitimate government collapse, was of greater significance.

The Anglo-French *entente*

Grey aimed to ensure that Britain should not be without friends to stand by her if the peace of Europe was shattered by the new stronger Germany. It was therefore axiomatic with him that 'what determines foreign policy ... is the question of sea power'. Britain would need friends because she no longer ruled supreme — hence the renewal of the Anglo-Japanese Alliance in 1905 and 1911. At the same time he was determined to pursue friendly relations with Germany provided Germany would acquiesce in friendly relations between the *Entente* powers. Thus, by not committing herself, the balance would be upheld since Britain would be able to throw her diplomatic weight behind the attacked and against the aggressor as a neutral arbiter. Such was the position that Grey occupied in pursuit of British interests.

Grey inherited Lansdowne's *Entente* with Cambon which removed colonial disputes in Egypt and obtained for France the promise of diplomatic support in Morocco. It is debatable whether the secret articles signed by Lansdowne would have been signed by Grey had he made the *Entente*. They provided for the respective spheres of influence of France and Spain in case the Sultan's government of Morocco should at any future time disintegrate. In March 1905 the Kaiser had landed at Tangier pressing for an international conference to settle the problem of France's penetration of Morocco, and this had already caused the resignation of the hawkish Delcassé, a humiliating sacrifice to avoid German invasion. Hence Grey was determined to make some sort of gesture because he saw the *Entente* as necessary to prevent Germany making 'mischief between other countries by saying poisoned things to one about the other. It is the lees left by Bismarck that still fouled the cup.'[1]

At the same time Grey was faced with the threat of Russia gravitating towards Germany with the Bjorkoe Treaty which threatened the Franco-Russian Alliance and might isolate Britain in Europe. The conference at Algeciras would require some sign from Britain that the *Entente* was to be taken seriously. Cambon saw Grey twice on 10 and 31 January 1906, to clarify Britain's position. The real issue of these conversations was not whether Britain would give France diplomatic support at the conference, but whether she would support France in arms if Germany pushed things to a war. In essence Grey's reply, that Britain could not pledge herself to military support unless France was wantonly attacked and then British support was only 'probable', was his position until August 1914. This reply was seen as significantly different from that of Lansdowne, who had said that if there was war between Germany and France over Morocco, 'Public feeling would force the government to fight for France.'[2] It is not, however, different from the reply Salisbury might have given had he been in this situation. Grey's full report of the interview is worth quoting:

> The French Ambassador asked me today Jan 10th whether in the event of an attack by Germany upon France arising out of the Morocco difficulty, France could rely upon the armed support of England.
>
> I said I could not answer this question … all I could promise was diplomatic support now. M. Cambon said he did not believe that there would be war, but that there would be no danger of war if the German Emperor knew that we should fight to help France. I said that I thought the German Emperor probably did expect this; but that it was one thing to let it be supposed in Germany that we should join in a war; it was a different thing to take an engagement to France to do it; it would be a very grave mistake to make a promise of that kind till one was absolutely certain it would be fulfilled.

Britain's military conversations would ensure that if attacked by Germany, France would have a speedy formal treaty with Britain. Germany knew that if she were the aggressor over the Morocco affair France could count on the support of Britain. This meant that there was no need for a formal alliance As to France's worry that Germany might attack within a matter of 'minutes', it would be so serious that an agreement would have to be put in writing. This course of action would not be acceptable in Britain because it would be too binding. Against this is the view that Grey had already bound Britain to France by the secret military conversations, so that as far as armed support for France in a war against Germany, Grey's 'no' began to sound more and more like a 'yes' to the French.

The constraints on British policy

Because Grey failed to avert war after nine years he has been criticised by two opposing schools: one school says he should not have made agreements at all but returned to splendid isolation; the other maintains that he should have converted the *Entente* into alliances. Supporters of the first school feared war with Germany and believed that Britain alone could remain superior at sea. But Grey could not afford to watch France or Russia be pulled into the orbit of Germany, which was in danger of happening in December 1905, when he came to office, because of the Bjorkoe agreement and Germany's threat to divide the *Entente Cordiale* over Morocco. German dominance on the continent was a real possibility and British isolation would not be a welcome prospect against a Europe united under German hegemony. Thus Grey foresaw war if the *entente* with France was broken up:

> If ... by ... some misfortune or blunder our *entente* with France were broken up, France will have to make her own terms with Germany. And Germany will again be in a position to keep us on bad terms with France and Russia and to make herself predominant on the Continent. Then, sooner or later, there will be war between us and Germany, in which much else may be involved.[3]

Apart from the threat of Germany it must be remembered, too, that the agreements with France and Russia had been originally undertaken to avoid the possibility of war with those two countries in the Upper Nile, Egypt and Afghanistan and Persia respectively. This was, then, the context of the rise of German power.

On the other hand the 'Firm Alliance' school maintain that Germany would never have hazarded war if there had been a firm alliance between France and Britain. Apart from the arguments advanced above that Germany knew that Britain would support France if Germany was the aggressor, two other reasons are advanced against this course of action: Grey could not make such an alliance because Parliament would not have agreed to it (the constitutional argument); and he would not do it because he was afraid it might encourage France or Russia to attack Germany first. Grey argued that the very uncertainty of the British position acted as a restraint. But was it a restraint on Germany? It was argued that alliances with Russia and France would have been more likely to have precipitated war by increasing Germany's feelings of encirclement. Germany complained of encirclement anyway, but she almost certainly encircled herself by alienating France over Alsace–Lorraine, estranging Russia by her support of Austria-Hungary's anti-Slav policy in the Balkans, and Britain by building a rival fleet.

The Naval race and Agadir

Grey's main concern was with Britain's seapower, which is why he was prepared to concentrate the fleet in home waters in 1912, allowing the French to patrol the Mediterranean. But he made it clear once again to the French that Britain still remained uncommitted to France. Ironically, Germany threatened British naval supremacy only to keep her neutral while France was crushed, but its very existence rendered neutrality impossible, as can be seen from the promises to France on 31 July, 1914. Both McKenna and Grey threatened to resign during the naval race with Germany, which led to the Dreadnought building programme in effect going ahead. What Grey was aiming at in his dealings with Germany was:

> to be friends … if possible, not to resist her expansion in Asiatic Turkey, but not to become dependent on her by losing control of the sea.[4]

This was illustrated after the Bosnian Crisis when Grey's policy of reviving the Concert of Europe received a rebuff from Austria and Germany, so that during the Agadir Crisis of 1911 Grey was forced to emphasise that the British attitude over Morocco was not 'a disinterested one'. But Grey resisted the French invitation to send a French and English warship to Agadir while at the same time permitting Lloyd George to make the Mansion House speech to emphasise the seriousness of the situation. This seemed to achieve the desired effect in Germany after the euphoria of the 'Panther Spring', and it illustrates Grey's attempts at balancing the threat of force with an adequate degree of 'impartiality'.

Sarajevo and after

The Sarajevo assassination had little effect on Britain, apart from producing sympathy for the Austrians (nothing was known at the time of the famous German 'blank cheque' of 5 July): on 23 July 1914 Lloyd George was arguing in the Commons for economies in the next budget on the grounds that relations with Germany had never been better. Until 2 August it was an open question as to what England would do. Germany had declared war on Russia because she had refused to demobilise. Grey had been criticised for not putting pressure on

Russia, but the Germans had refused an international conference along the same lines as that of 1913 to settle the Balkan Wars, and Russia was far less prepared than Germany for a war. Germany had also declared war on France. Grey was convinced that the sequel to German dominance on the Continent would be another war in which Britain would have a much harder job of it. But his primary objective was to keep the Cabinet together:

> I used to hope that I was meant to keep the country out of war. But perhaps my real business was to bring her into it unitedly.

Although he had asked both the French and Germans on 31 July whether in the event of war they would respect Belgian neutrality, and Germany had refused to reveal her plans, this would not have been enough to bring Britain into the war on 31 July, since the Cabinet was still divided. It was only on the morning of 2 August that Grey was authorised to assure the French that if the German fleet came up the Channel or through the North Sea undertaking hostile operations against the French coast, the British fleet would give all the protection in its power, subject to receiving support of Parliament.

And it was only on the day after Sunday 2 August, when news came in of the ultimatum to Belgium, that the Cabinet now sanctioned mobilisation. In the afternoon of 3 August Grey told the Commons how he had worked for peace. He made it clear that there was no technically-binding agreement to France despite the military conversations, the distribution of the fleets since 1912, and the pledge to hold the Channel, and as for any moral obligation: 'Let every man look into his own heart, his own feelings and construe the extent of the obligation for himself.' Finally he turned to Belgium placing it within the context of German domination of the continent, which he saw as the consequence of Britain keeping out of a war. The House approved entry into the war. Grey had failed to stop war, but he had succeeded in taking Britain united into it.

Notes
(1) Letter to Roosevelt (December 1906).
(2) Metterich to his government (3 January 1906).
(3) Letter to Roosevelt (December 1906).
(4) Letter to Sir Rennel Rodd (1913).

Sam Merry is a postgraduate student at the University of Southampton.

Jessica Saraga
Examiner's report

Jessica Saraga advises on essay construction using here a sample essay on Gladstone's Irish Home Rule Bill of 1886.

The question below is a standard one on nineteenth-century British history. That does not make it an easy one, though. It is rather deceptively straighforward, and gives you no clues in its wording about how to break it up and organise a plan. Before you read through this answer written by 'Sean', see if you can come up with your own plan. Sean wrote his essay early on in his A-level studies. When he came to sit his A-level papers he might well have answered it differently. He writes fluently, but tends to skim the surface of ideas without going into them enough. This means that although his answer is relevant, it is not always entirely convincing. Try to suggest to yourself as you read it what other explanation or information is needed to strengthen Sean's answer.

Question

Why did Gladstone fail to get Home Rule for Ireland in 1886?

The Liberal leader, William Gladstone, was determined that Ireland should have Home Rule, seeing it was 'morally right.' Unfortunately for Gladstone not everyone shared his point of view and the bill was rejected and thrown out of Parliament. This was a crushing blow for Gladstone and the Liberal party as it split them.

Your introduction is a vital part of your essay. It can signal to your reader straight away whether you have understood the question, and whether you have a good idea of how to set about answering it. Sean's is an interesting introduction which manages to suggest something of the importance of the Home Rule issue in the late nineteenth century and Gladstone's passionate concern for it. Sean also alerts us to the effect of the bill's rejection on the fortunes of the Liberal Party, which adds a nice sense of drama here, though it isn't, in fact, directly relevant to the question. What Sean hasn't done here, which he should have done, is to refer to any reasons why Gladstone failed to get Home Rule for Ireland. This, after all, is the whole point of the question. Part of the advice from Sean's teachers was: 'You should begin with a clear account of what you consider the overriding reason(s) for the failure of the bill, and then argue from there in detail.'

I'd also like to comment on Sean's use of quotation marks. Is there a difference between something being 'morally right' and something being morally right? Does Sean mean that to Gladstone Home Rule appeared morally right, but to some other people it didn't? This is what he goes on to say later, so it looks as though the quotation marks are superfluous. It's always much better, anyway, to be explicit about your meaning, rather than hinting at it through quotation marks.

The Home Rule Bill proposed that a Parliament would be established in Dublin and deal with Irish affairs only, while customs, defence and foreign affairs would be looked after by the Imperial Parliament. The Irish executive would be appointed by the Lord Lieutenant of Ireland, indirectly by Britain. The Irish Parliament would have no say in their policing and judicial matters for at least ten years. The bill also laid down that Ireland was to bear the cost of about one fifteenth of the National Debt.

Sean is quite right to explain what was in the Home Rule Bill, which he does without comment. He's going to need these facts to refer back to in presenting his case later on. However, again quite rightly, he doesn't let the facts take over and run his essay for him. Facts should be used to illustrate or support your points, but they won't make your points for you on their own. Sean gets credit for these facts when he goes on to use them in his argument later; if he's left them as they are here, he wouldn't have got much credit for them at all.

Gladstone hoped that he could appeal to the British people's moral sense. He argued that Ireland was a nation, and must be allowed to solve its own problems. Furthermore he told the British people that the Irish themselves overwhelmingly wanted Home Rule. This was not entirely true as the strong Protestant population in the North around Ulster did not want to be separated from Britain, nor did they want to be ruled by 'Catholic Irish peasants'. The Ulster question was a big stumbling block for Gladstone as he heard Lord Randolph Churchill say 'Ulster will fight and Ulster will be right.' Ulster was determined to stay part of the Union. In fact many 'Home Rulers' and Irish Nationalists felt that Gladstone's Bill was wrong in that the British Parliament could pass heavy taxation onto Ireland without an Irish MP to question it — 'taxation without representation'. Furthermore the Irish Nationalists were angry that they had no control over their police or judges.

This is where Sean comes back to the moral issue, but he also mixes in the Ulster question and Irish anger about not being given control over the police and judiciary. It would have been better to keep these issues separate.

The quotation marks are much in evidence again here. Sean includes one accurate use of them in his quotation from Lord Randolph Churchill, and one inaccurate use with his 'taxation without representation', which as far as I can see isn't any different from taxation without representation. The quotation marks around 'Home Rulers' seem to suggest that this is a nickname, not an official name — in which case Sean doesn't need to say 'Home Rulers' and Irish Nationalists. But it's the quotation marks around 'Catholic Irish peasants' which seem to be doing the most work. What are they suggesting? Were the Catholic Irish really peasants? All of them? Is this therefore an example of Protestant prejudice? Sean is asking his quotation marks to raise all these questions for him, when he should be dealing with them himself.

> The Conservatives led by Lord Salisbury disliked the bill intensely, and strongly opposed it. Lord Salisbury told a conference that the Irish were not fit to rule themselves and that giving Ireland independence would encourage other parts of the Empire to ask for Home Rule. He was worried that British security could be affected because this bill would encourage political violence and a working-class revolt.

Here Sean is beginning to cram too much information into too little space. He should refer to the conference by name, and say a bit more about the Conservative concern for the British Empire. He needs to explain that the Conservatives wanted to avoid other parts of the Empire regarding Irish Home Rule as a precedent for their own future independence. He should also explain why Salisbury might think the bill would encourage political violence and working-class revolt; the government feared that the working class might see the bill as the government's response to Irish violence, and therefore be encouraged to use violence to further their own causes. One thing he misses when discussing the Conservative response to the bill is that another reason why the Conservatives opposed it was simply because Gladstone was for it. They wanted him out, and this looked like a good way to defeat him.

> In fact it is true to say that much of the British populace felt that the Irish were stupid and incapable of looking after themselves, and many people agreed with Salisbury. Some of the strongest criticism came from inside the Liberal party from Joseph Chamberlain, a radical. He argued that the bill had many inconsistencies like trusting the Irish but not giving them control of their police force. Chamberlain and the radicals now saw their chance of getting rid of Gladstone and so voted with the Conservatives. Another group who left the Liberal party was the Whigs who for many years felt

that the Liberal leadership was becoming too radical in their views and the Home Rule bill was the last straw. The two groups called themselves Unionists and voted with the Conservatives.

Gladstone went around the country trying to gain the public's confidence, but it proved unsuccessful and the bill was thrown out by Parliament and then the public.

Here Sean would have done well to make more distinction between the problems created by opposition to Home Rule inside the Liberal Party and those created by opposition in the country at large. Opposition inside the Liberal Party meant that Gladstone could not command a majority for the bill in Parliament. Opposition in the country meant that Gladstone had no option of calling an election on the Home Rule question to try to get a bigger majority. Then Sean could link up the two areas of opposition, by suggesting that Liberal Unionists were encouraged in their opposition by their knowledge of the feeling in the country. He also needs to go further into the reasons for the Liberal Unionists disliking the bill, explaining, for example, that Joseph Chamberlain shared the Conservatives' concern for the Empire.

Finally, it can be said that Gladstone failed to get Home Rule for Ireland in 1886 because of the British public's prejudice against the Irish, fears that the Empire might be split, criticism from the Conservative and Liberal party of the bill, and Gladstone's miscalculation of British opinion.

Sean is quite rightly now trying to sum up his ideas in a conclusion, and his conclusion does have the merit of referring back to the question and suggesting an answer to it. But instead of just using repeated ideas and running them into a list, Sean should try to probe a bit further and suggest a rank order of reasons why Gladstone failed to get Home Rule in 1886, or at least to pick out a reason which he thinks was particularly important. Alternatively, he might draw out of all this the generalised point that there was just too much opposition, both amongst the politicians and amongst the general public, some based on sincerely held views but much of it, particularly amongst the public, based on ignorance and prejudice. He might also very briefly point out that even if the bill had passed the Commons, it would never have passed the House of Lords. There is always a bit more to say in a conclusion than just to repeat what you've already said.

General comments

There is never just one right way of answering a question. Scriptmarkers are constantly surprised by how many different valid ways candidates come up with of approaching the same question. If you devised your own plan before reading Sean's answer, you may find that it is totally different from his. But as long as you can justify your plan, it is likely to be a sound one. The Irish Question in late nineteenth-century and early twentieth-century Britain is an interesting topic not simply because it was such a major concern of Gladstone's. It was also crucial to the changes in party alignments in this period when, with the defection of the Liberal Unionists, the Conservatives adopted their modern style of the Conservative and Unionist Party. What is more, Ireland was regarded as a pawn in the party political game. The Conservatives talked of 'playing the Orange card' when invoking Ulster Unionists to resist Home Rule in 1912, just as Lord Randolph Churchill had done in 1886. The Irish Nationalist MPs themselves were a force in non-Irish affairs too, since so often they held the balance of power between the two main parties, being able to choose which one to sustain in government by their support.

In focusing just on 1886, this question is very specific, demanding accurate and detailed knowledge of this particular year. A broader, background knowledge of the Irish Question is also a prerequisite for answering the question, since it would be impossible to write confidently on 1886 without it. Sean's answer does manage to convey that he is aware of the longer-term importance of the issue as well as its importance for Gladstone's Third Ministry. Altogether he does end up with some credit. He needs to demonstrate rather more understanding of the concerns of the Conservatives and the Liberal Unionists on the Irish Question, and he needs to be bolder in his final analysis of the reasons why Home Rule failed in 1886. However, he has clearly thought about the question and the result is a fluent and concise answer.

Jessica Saraga has wide experience as a sixth-form teacher and examiner.

Index

Aberdeen, Lord 13
Agadir Crisis 1911, 120
Agriculture 52, 55, 87
Amalgamated Society of
    Engineers 86, 89
Arch, Joseph 85, 87
Artisans' Dwelling Act 1875, 62
Asquith, H. H. 112
Austria-Hungary 116, 120

Balfour A J, 73
Balkans, The 32, 59, 117
Bentinck, Lord George 56–7
Berlin, Congress of 58
Boer War 1899–1902, 72, 75–82,
    114
Booth, Charles 103
Bosnian Crisis 1908, 115
Bradford Labour Union 95
British Empire 11, 72–3, 75, 80,
    114, 124
Broadhurst, Henry 90

Campbell-Bannerman, Sir Henry
    79
Catholicism 11, 45, 47, 61, 88, 96,
    123
Chamberlain, Joseph 32, 63–4,
    66–74, 76, 83, 115, 124
Church of England 11, 15
Church of Ireland 27–9
Churchill, Lord Randolph 20, 33,
    51, 62, 124
Combination Acts 85–7
Clarion, The 97
Conservative Party 13, 16, 20,
    22–4, 39, 46, 48, 51, 61, 64–6,
    112, 124–5
Corn Laws, repeal of 13, 54, 55–7
Corrupt Practices Act 1883, 18
Cross, R.A. 62, 64

Davison, Emily Wilding 109
Davitt, Michael 37, 39

Derby, Earl of 21–2, 28, 51, 63, 57
Disraeli, Benjamin 5, 10, 16, 21,
    28, 51, 53–61

Easter Rising 1916, 49
Entente Cordiale 114, 117, 119

Fawcett, Millicent 110
Fenians, The 29, 36–7, 42
Foreign Policy 1894–1914, 114–21
Forster's Education Act 1870, 9,
    15, 16, 68
France 114, 117–21
franchise, the 19–26, 63, 94
Free trade 12, 73, 83, 104–5,
    109–13
Friendly Societies 84, 86, 88

Germany 9, 83, 94, 114, 116,
    118–21
Grand National Consolidated
    Trade Union 86–8
Gladstone, William Ewert 9–10,
    11–17, 19, 25, 27–34, 38–42, 51,
    58–9, 69–70, 122
Grey, Sir Edward 114–18, 120–1

Harcourt, Sir William 104
Hardie, Kier 93, 95, 96, 100
Home Rule for Ireland 12, 16, 23,
    30–4, 35–42, 46, 48, 61–3, 70–1,
    95, 107, 122–5
Hyndman, H. M. 99

Independent Labour Party 23, 84,
    93–101
Industrial Revolution 85–6
Imperialism 72–3
Irish Coercian Act 1881 38, 56
Irish famine 36–7
Irish Land League 31, 37
Irish Land War 32, 38, 41
Irish Nationalists 20, 22, 34, 45–7,
    49–50, 123

Kilmainham Treaty 38
Kitchener, Lord 77–8

Labour Party 5, 7, 26, 34, 64, 84, 112
Labour Representation Committee 93, 101
laissez-faire 12, 102
Liberal Party 9, 11–17, 23–4, 40, 46, 49, 58, 61, 63, 67, 83–4, 95, 112, 122–4
Lloyd George, David 50, 66, 72, 83, 106–7, 112, 120
London Dock Strike 1889, 87, 96, 98

MacDonald, Ramsay 93
Mann, Tom 90
Mill, John Stuart 25, 111
Morris, William 98
Municipal Socialism 68, 103

National Agricultural Labourers' Union 85
National Insurance Act 1911 105
National Union of Women's Suffrage Societies 111
New Liberalism 7, 102–8
New Model Unions 86–8
'New Unionism' 85–92
Nonconformity 14, 28, 67–8

O'Connell, Daniel 27
O'Connor, T.P. 40
Old Age Pensions 106
O'Shea, Katharine 41–2
Osborne Judgement 1909 64

Palmerston, Lord 9, 13, 16, 59, 61
Pankhursts 109–10, 112
Parnell, Charles Stewart 30, 35–42, 67
Parliamentary reforms in the 1880s 18–26
Partition of Ireland 44, 46–50
Peel, Sir Robert 12, 55–6, 58
'People's Budget' 1909, 107

Phoenix Park murders 1882, 39, 67
Primrose League 6, 23
Protestantism 47, 61, 63, 64, 88, 96

Radical Programme 69–70
Redistribution Act 1885, 18, 21, 23, 39, 63
Reform Act 1867, 5, 15, 18, 23, 58, 67
Reform Act 1884, 5, 18, 23, 39
Representation of the People Act 1918, 109
Rowntree, Seebohm 103
Russia 59, 62, 94, 114–15

Salisbury, Lord 20, 51, 53, 65, 73, 116, 124
Samuel, Herbert 105
Secret Ballot 1872 18
Smiles, Samuel 89
Social Democratic Federation 6, 99–100
'splendid isolation' 114–17, 119
State intervention 6–7, 103–4, 107

Taff Vale Judgement 1901 64
Tariff reform 73, 83, 104
'Tory Democracy' 61–6
Trade Boards Act 1909, 106
Trade Disputes Act 1906, 105
Trade Union Act 1871, 15
Trade Union Act 1913, 105
Trades Union Congress 6, 85, 94

Ulster 44–9, 123, 126
Unionists 40, 45, 49, 63–5, 71, 73, 126
Unemployment 90–1, 106

Vereeniging, Treaty of 80

Wellington, Duke of 53, 56
Women's Social and Political Union 110
Women's Suffrage 25, 109–13
World War, First 1914–18, 26, 34, 47, 73, 112